UNITY LIBRARY 8 ARCHIVES
Hope in this world,
BR 121.2 .B283

0 0051 0031 51i 5

C0-AWD-649

HOPE in This World

Books by Wesley C. Baker
Published by The Westminster Press

Hope in This World

Believer in Hell

The Open End of Christian Morals

More Than a Man Can Take: A Study of Job

HOPE
in This World

by WESLEY C. BAKER

THE WESTMINSTER PRESS

Philadelphia

UNITY SCHOOL LIBRARY
Unity Village
Lee's Summit, Missouri 64063

COPYRIGHT © MCMLXX THE WESTMINSTER PRESS

All rights reserved—no part of this book may be reproduced in any form without permission in writing from the publisher, except by a reviewer who wishes to quote brief passages in connection with a review in magazine or newspaper.

Scripture quotations from the Revised Standard Version of the Bible are copyright, 1946 and 1952, by the Division of Christian Education of the National Council of Churches, and are used by permission.

STANDARD BOOK No. 664–24864–0

LIBRARY OF CONGRESS CATALOG CARD No. 78–94450

PUBLISHED BY THE WESTMINSTER PRESS ®
PHILADELPHIA, PENNSYLVANIA

PRINTED IN THE UNITED STATES OF AMERICA

To Becky, and Ernie, and Tim—

So sorry, beloved offspring. I can't guarantee a thing about your safety, or happiness, or success. The future is too unpredictable, uncontrollable, mysterious. The world is still so young it has many turmoils yet to go through. Some of them may have the backlash of a thousand tornadoes.

Come to think of it, it's better that way after all. With hope, who needs a guarantee?

PREFACE

Easter Sunday in New York City. Bright, clear, noisy, smelly, lively, dingy. It's only a few minutes' walk from Riverside Church to the Cathedral of St. John the Divine, if you skirt Columbia University. If you choose, you can easily take part in the action at both places, possibly the two biggest churches in American Protestantism.

At Riverside, all is clean and proper, almost clinically flawless in order and impressiveness. The music seems to have no limits of dynamic expression; the preaching is a model of literary lucidity. After the service, with spirits quickened by the resurrection story, we embark on the short walk. On Broadway there is the usual sprinkling of shuffling, unseeing, unsmiling humanity, the jostling and shoving around the subway entrance, and the speeding taxis running a race for survival of the fastest. At 114th Street an abandoned car rests on wheelless axles, its hood open like a gasping crocodile. Forty feet beyond, an old woman steps laboriously over the body of a sleeping drunk. Two little boys play hide-and-seek behind up-turned garbage cans. At Amsterdam Avenue, a fender-bender traffic accident is about to blossom into a wing-ding of a fistfight.

At the steps of the cathedral, a tourist bus unloads fifty gawking rubbernecks and a uniformed guide with a bullhorn, who cajoles his flock to make way through the waiting choir and clergy to the far door. An ambulance shrieks by, three buses fill the intersection with diesel exhaust, and Harlem lies sullenly just beyond the park.

But the service begins withal, and the great doors are opened. The bishop knocks, the trumpets sound, and again the majesty of the resurrection is told. Splendor. Squalor. Dignity. Misery. Inspiration. Dehumanization.

Every day is Easter Day in New York.

With this book, a cycle of five is completed. It wasn't planned that way; it just happened. Probably the five represent a review of the important themes that twenty-one years of proclaiming the gospel laid bare. The church militant, the triumph in suffering, responsible morality, and the defeated lostness of depression—all simply had to lead to the real issue: hope. It was a pilgrimage unaware, and even the climb up the cathedral steps has for its background music the dissonance of all of us squalling our own unharmonized wails. Then someone intones the story of death defused and life affirmed, and even the vacant staring eyes of the unfriendly become objects of love. That's what it's all about. No damned mushroom cloud can blot out the sun forever, nor ever destroy the Real. To believe in this world, and to live in it in hope, is to want to tell it everywhere.

W.C.B.

New York, New York
Easter, 1969

CONTENTS

1

It's Another One of Those Times When We Need a Good Word

This writing is a subjective, emotional, almost involuntary burst of *hope*.

Sure, this world's a mess. I'll buy that. I remember only too well the words of the radio commentator in the depressingly grim days of September, 1939. "We learn from history," he sighed, "that we learn nothing from history."

But I can't buy despair. I've been through my own time of stumbling in the Valley of the Shadow, and the whole experience spoke a word to me that I try here, ever so clumsily, to pass on to others.

The tee-off came, I think, on a train from Philadelphia to New York. Or it may have been on a bus from Sacramento to San Francisco. At any rate, my seatmate was a tired businessman prone to a weary pessimism. Across the aisle, two pretty young things just past the teenybopper stage displayed rather attractive legs in loud-colored net stockings topped by refreshingly short shifts. In front sat two LOL's (Herb Caen's term for "little old ladies") commiserating on their Medicare and pension shortshrifts. Behind us were two Pfc.'s en route back to the base, dividing their attention between the cross-aisle crossed legs and their own uncertain futures.

My ears rotated like the turning antennae of airport radar, catching only snatches of conversation from all directions, with little attempt or need for understanding the continuity.

"I don't know." Sighing, my elbow-rubbing executive friend slapped the newspaper to make it stay in the right place. "I just don't know. This latest international crisis is really going to hurt the stock market. It just keeps happening over and over." He shook his head and clucked his tongue with a one-cheek grimace. "Can't go on like this forever."

On the distaff side of the aisle the conversation was gushing in mighty treble waves. "And George turned and looked at me in that funny walleyed way of his, and he said, 'Why should we get married? We've got everything now we're ever going to have. Why spoil it?' He isn't quite sure yet whether he will let himself be drafted or be a conscientious objector, and he thinks marriage would only be a handicap. So I said to him . . ."

From behind: "I put in to the CO for overseas duty right out of training camp, hoping to get Germany or something like that. But he said that the chances for Vietnam are 99 out of 100 and it didn't make any difference what I wanted. I know I gotta go sometime, but y'know, I think a system that makes a guy go into a fight he doesn't understand . . ."

From one LOL to another: "Do you know, I was visiting my daughter just last summer when that horrible race riot broke out, and we were only about twenty blocks away. I am just as sure as I can be that it was all incited by Communists. In fact, I heard Dr. McIntire last Tuesday morning prove that the whole turmoil is the result of a worldwide conspiracy, and some of our very own leaders and ministers and churches and politicians are responsible! Why, just *anything* could happen!"

"Really? You were right there? Of course, I always suspected that those Commies were out to destroy us by stirring up the poor colored folk. They've always been so happy! But you were an eyewitness, and you know for sure! I just can't wait to tell my friends . . ."

She was jammed off my listening frequency by my salesman friend. "Didja see the Dow-Jones index this morning? Up two and a half. Won't stay, though. Business is sick. Lots of money changing hands, but it's all spinning off in inflation. I figure we got maybe another fifty years."

"Fifty years until what?" I asked.

"Until the whole sheboom goes down like a house of cards."

"You mean the economy?"

"I mean the whole country. The way we're going now, with labor unions squeezing the blood out of corporate profits, and the Commies pushing the niggers to burn our cities, we just don't have any future. No future at all."

Several other questions tried to surface in my mind but the listening gear, hungry for a good word, had tuned in again across the aisle.

"When you get your apartment, do you want to have a baby?"

"I dunno. At first, I thought it would be real groovy—I always liked to play with dolls. I know George wouldn't mind; I could have a baby whenever I want. But what's the future in it? Things are getting pretty grim, and I don't know if it would be fair to the little tyke. You just don't know which way things are going to go—know what I mean?"

"I'd like to have a baby. I think it would be fun. I could get the little girl down the hall to sit with him while I go out on dates."

"But what if he got sick and you had to take time off

from work? You gotta think of those things, you know."

"Yeah, I guess you're right. And like you said, the world isn't in too good a shape right now."

"Yeah."

The theme passed from strings to brass, as it were, where the soldiers took it up.

"I went to radio school, thinking I could go into some kind of electronics maintenance work when I got out, but it turned out to be too hard."

"Too hard? Whaddya mean?"

"They wanted me to go to a sixteen-week basic, then a six-month secondary before getting a T-3 rate. Hell, I can get that in half the time driving trucks in the supply pool."

"But there's damn good money in electronics in civilian life."

"Pay's just as good driving trucks, maybe better. Don't forget good old Jimmy and the Teamsters' Union. Some of those guys are doing better than lawyers or doctors."

"But didn't you really want to go into electronics?"

"Sure did. Lot better than pushing the big rigs. But ya gotta do what pays the best with the least trouble nowadays."

Then after a pause in which I had really intended to tune them out, but somehow couldn't, came the cryptic footnote.

"No use doing anything you don't get paid for. It's a pretty crappy old world."

". . . and furthermore," my seatmate droned on, "the next administration is going to be so tied up in labor conflicts and Black Power riots that business will be hurt real bad. Then just watch money tighten up!"

At this juncture I realized I was getting a little bit depressed. My eavesdropping only seemed to bring in the signals of despair. Perhaps my fellow travelers were tired,

14

I thought. Or they really do feel otherwise, but the cooped-up situation brought out the worst. I decided to force a change of subject.

Turning to the gentleman at my side, I spoke in a voice loud enough for all to hear. "Doesn't it give you a thrill to realize you are living in the generation that put a man on the moon—and may even reach Mars?"

The proverbial lead balloon hit the floor with a thud. Mr. Stock Market stared embarrassedly out the window, then put his head in both hands. The soldiers behind snorted, "Oh, brr-other!" Across the aisle, one bit of fluff whispered to the other, "I hope he's the first to go!"

Up front, my words were taken more seriously. Two long, baleful, incredulous, blank stares over the shoulder in my direction were followed by this conversation: "Why in heaven's name should anyone want to go to the moon?"

"Gracious, yes! It's already definitely known that those places are crawling with ugly murderous creatures."

The failure to inject a bit of cheer into the air impressed me. I realized I had tuned in on a cross section of contemporary thought, given out in packages as profound and revealing as any philosopher's writings. There was indeed an element of futility about the present and apprehension about the future that made every generation present tend to be cynical. It seemed to me that there were many wonderful reasons for hope, but this mind-set didn't seem to want to be troubled with facts.

Oh, well, I sighed. You can't win them all. So I tilted my seat back and tried to get some sleep.

Later, perhaps the same week, I was in a restaurant in the Haight-Ashbury section of San Francisco. Or was it the East Village of New York? Anyway, at the next table, fortunately downwind, sat a young couple whose bodies had known neither soap nor razor nor laundered garments in many a moon. While he (I think it was the he) strummed a guitar, she sang:

> *I turned to my friend for bread,*
> *He gave me a stone.*
> *I turned to my leader for kindness,*
> *He increased my taxes.*
> *I turned to my country for a cause,*
> *It gave me a gun and taught me to kill.*
> *I turned to God for love,*
> *He said it was all gone, to come back tomorrow.*
> *There won't be any tomorrow.*
> *I'm going to keep on loving,*
> *We all have our thing.*

It may have been the lighthearted hopelessness, or the winsome grief, or the appealing loneliness, or sheer curiosity that made me go sit and talk with them.

"I take it you are a little pessimistic about the present order," I started off questioningly.

"Are you kidding?" I think the respondent was the girl. It wasn't too easy to be certain in the dim light. "Man, there isn't any present order. Just chaos."

"Yeah, man," chimed in her partner, "dry dust. Nothingsville."

"Well"—I thought I had a fascinating tack—"what do you intend to do about it?"

"Just stay out of it, man. It's the only thing to do." He strummed the guitar softly and began to hum.

"That's ridiculous," I snorted. "You live in this world just as much as any of us, and you have to deal with it. You just can't declare yourself totally irresponsible while the rest of us are carrying your loads!"

Down went the guitar on the table, and it was then I realized that these young folk were no imbeciles. "Look," he said, earnestly glaring through his Louis Pasteur glasses, "there's you squares and there's us groovies, right?"

"Right!" I said, though my mind was still working out the implications of his terminology.

"We know that ours is a subculture, and like all subcultures it won't take over the world. But we just can't dig the artificiality and hypocrisy of the square world. It pollutes the soul and degrades the person. Right?"

"Well, in some ways—maybe. But it has its good points."

"Name one." This from the girl-type.

"Never mind that," interrupted her man. "We just don't dig it. We've gotta be ourselves—y'know? We've got to live out our thing. And being caught in the bag of walking around faceless like you conforming ghosts, pretending we don't hate and yet taking part in class cruelty, just isn't our thing. So we live as we do."

"And how is that?"

"As though any day, any minute, may be the very last. It's only those who worry about the future and become all sorts of insecure that get all balled up with hate. If you have no future, you can be freed to be a person of love."

"You don't think there's going to be much of a future for civilization as we know it?"

"I couldn't care less. If the world doesn't blow itself up pretty damned soon, it's going to *mediocre* itself into nowhere."

So much for them. I didn't even pay for their coffee, as I had originally intended. If they had no future to plan for, they could jolly well spend all they had right now.

But of course, their words haunted me. We do indeed live in an apocalyptic age, with the future a big oblong threatening blur. Some of us decry it, some fight it, some just give up, crawl into a hole, and pull it in after them.

It was that very night, of all times, that I picked up a magazine to read the following juicy tidbit:

America's atomic scientists feel that the world is in greater danger of nuclear annihilation than ever before. As a symbolic indication, the hands of the clock shown on the cover of the *Bulletin of the Atomic Scientists* have been moved five minutes closer to midnight. The graphic clock, appearing on the cover for two decades, had indicated twelve minutes to midnight since 1963.

Eugene Rabinowitch, editor of the bulletin, points out that the clock serves "as a symbol of the shadow of disaster under which all mankind is living since the development of atomic weapons." He says that the reason for changing the clock's hands was not associated with any particular event but indicated a trend characterized by increased violence and nationalism. (*Presbyterian Life*, Feb. 15, 1968, p. 21.)

No doubt about it. When you put together the fragments of opinion from the many very different sources of modern thought, you come up with a general "end of the era" psychology. A surprisingly universally held, mostly unspoken assumption seems to prevail among hippies and LOL's, privileged and poor, cabbies and scientists, that as a world we've had it. These last few decades of what we so lovingly used to call "progress" were so fast and bumpy and unpleasant that the only comfortable thing to think is that the journey is almost over.

Not that it's a gloomy shadow over all that we do. Buildings are going up everywhere; schools are being erected and staffed and administered. The stock market stays open and continues to prosper; airplanes get bigger and faster and arrive on time. It's just that we don't look forward with the same gusto with which we look sideways. We're not a people without hope; we're a people who suspect that the present may have a helluva lot more security in it than the future, so we just don't let hope get in the way. It's not really absent, but its presence isn't the outstanding reality of the now.

An honest amateur psychologist would say that we are covering frustration with fantasy; that hope, or at least a certain positive affirmation in the next stages of history, is an element of health. Or is even that a naïve Pollyannaism that is out of step with modern life? A person must muse quite a bit to find where his own integrity and value structure bring him out. One night, reading the *New York Post,* I came across these lines by Harriet Van Horne:

In times of trembling uncertainty, I admire people who build houses, breed babies, plant trees and tuck away precious heirlooms for unborn grandchildren. With the subject of nuclear warfare edging back into the news, it takes courage even to take advantage of a "big money-saving" five year subscription. Doing all these things is an affirmation of life. And the most valuable people in this world are those who say Yes! to life, no matter what. The people who, in the face of Vietnam and drug-dotty hippies and assorted Dr. Strangeloves roaming the corridors of power, still maintain a stubborn optimism about the human condition. It is this wild faith in the ultimate sanity of man that gives inner security. (*New York Post,* Jan. 16, 1968.)

Is it so crazy to think that history yet has a lot more in store for us than an imminent nothingsville? Is it a sign of sickness or of health to dream about living in a society that looks forward with expectant zeal? Is it passé to feel that there are long-range possibilities in every good development of a pleasant day?

The words of my youthful rebel friends in the café kept performing instant replay in my memory. It was easy to project that to my brave assertion, "There are many reasons for believing that the real issues of mankind are just getting under way," the retort would obviously be, "Name one."

Yes, name one. Document one bit of incontrovertible evidence. Without lapsing into a sickly out-of-this-world-liness, it just wasn't possible to counter the hard facts of nuclear horror potential, international danger, the widening gap between rich and poor, the long hot summers and increasing ghetto violence and brutality, and on and on. Try to match those with statistics from a UN agency about new developments in Soviet-American teamwork in oceanography, and feel as blah about the subject as I did.

No, I deny that I was depressed. That battle had already been fought and won on a different field. I was compulsively curious. It just seemed a damned shame that to enjoy a pleasant sunny day, which I frequently do, it was necessary to blot out of my mind the specter of upcoming history. Or, if I did insist on doing a little dreaming, it had to be framed by a mythological conditioning: "If there *is* such a world, it will be perfect . . ." More cautious realists who were addicted to a little unjustified hope were careful to build in an apologetic escape hatch: "Of course, the odds are against it, *but* if Yale is still there in the year 2000 . . ."

At the same time, I was carrying on a different life in a parallel column that I was keeping clinically separate. This was the continuous process of reading and research that is the order of the day for a professional man of any discipline today. Doctors must read their journals, buzz with their buddies, tote up the implications of their own experience. Lawyers must immerse themselves in digests, court decisions, bar associations (!), and so forth. My profession, that of clergyman, is carried out not only in the teaching atmosphere of pulpit and classroom but in the counseling chambers and by the sickbeds and in community organizations and peering through the meshed screens in prison visitors' cages. Just to keep the flow of enforcement material going through my support circuits requires reading in theology, Biblical studies, psychology, political history, philosophy, newspapers, and everything from Plato to *Playboy* in human dialogue.

It is an occupational hazard of my profession that no matter how consistent the practitioner is in keeping this traffic flowing, he can easily fall into the practice of pre-recording a vast storage of cerebral tapes that get stacked in a fading memory vault. When and if they are needed, the proper cartridge is slipped into the "play" position, and whatever was learned three months ago at some institute is poured out as a sermon illustration or a homey little point at a Rotary meeting. In the process of replay, the sound paths hardly ever get crossed up with the conversation with oneself in which faith and hopes and personal vulnerability appear.

That's why I say parallel but separate columns. As the movement of the world's greatest ideas went by me, I was looking on those ideas as usable commodities for being professionally effective. And yet on the other side of some invisible wall I was living on a starvation diet myself.

There was one place, however, where the barrier of separation was quite thin. I have always developed spinal chills at exposures to history. I'm one of those creeps who will stand before the statue of the minuteman at Concord Bridge in a driving rain and weep. What cathedrals do to some people, an ancient Indian cliff dwelling in Arizona will do for me. I was actually reluctant to enter the house in Vienna where Beethoven wrote his Sixth Symphony for fear my juvenile glee would embarrass my bored companions. The very thought of visiting the Holy Land someday is nearly unbearable.

This is probably why reading the Bible turns me on.

Just seeing how they did it, in their way and in their time, does spark across and affect the way I do it in my time. Or at least, their way becomes a live consideration. As a teen-age boy on the Mojave Desert of Southern California, I spent long hours absorbing the massive silence and sparkling clarity of the sheer openness, wondering if the young Moses in exile in a similar country was touched by the same feelings. Later, driving a gasoline truck across the more desolate parts of Nevada, I wondered if I could possibly ever understand the loneliness of Elijah as he sought out Horeb in the wilderness. As a student missionary in the south-of-Market district of San Francisco, I missed my desert security and wondered if the Israelites in Babylonian exile had tasted the same wine of homesickness.

It was the awesome contemporaneity and unapologetic humanity of the Bible that grabbed me. Remembering the words of Harry Emerson Fosdick, I found something for today in every page: "The old Book has moved into a new world. There are sharp contrasts between some ways of thinking in the Bible and our own. There is no use obscuring the fact. We would better set it out in the clear light and deal with it. . . . If there are new ways of approaching men's minds, new methods of argument and apologetic, let us have them. But we shall soon see that the old Book already knew the men we were talking about in its way."

But enough of that. If the Bible is anything other than a repository of religious insights, it is history. Not major world history, of course, but history nonetheless. The one undeniable dimension of it is its antiquity, and from there it becomes almost a family diary, in the sense that the "family" is a collection of related tribes that can become occasionally a nation and at other times a scattered, demoralized, and disorganized but still related people. The simple fact of a continuity through centuries of ancient times, lived alongside the great cultures of Egypt, Babylon, Syria, Greece, and Rome, gives this family record an authenticity of its own.

This may be what can be called the secular value of Biblical history. Whatever you may think of the religious idealism, the fact is that there was survival, and that alone is enough to make the whole story remarkable; and for those of us to whom the idea of survival is a major proposition, the Bible brings a rather powerful set of propositions worth considering.

In addition to all that, the culmination of the Biblical story is the appearance on the human scene of the Christian church, a shaper of culture and thought primarily for the Western world, and in some manner for all continents. Even though the canonical writings only introduce this community, carrying it through but a couple of generations, they reveal more of the characteristic fabric of this movement than most contemporary thinkers usually take time to understand. Not just because of my orientation in Christian thought, but also because of my immersion in the human bewilderments of the twentieth century, am I led to consider and discuss the whole ball of wax that is today's context in terms of the history reflected in the Bible, and in religious impressions.

I see now that this understanding of the significance of Biblical history is the first phase of my answer (intuitively found, rather than deliberately reasoned through) to the challenge to come up with hard-and-fast evidence for hope. Simply put, it occurs to me that I find myself looking at the present situation as a beginning to a new age because my forefathers in the faith did the same in their times, and the record proved them right. Admittedly, the whole thing so far is just that, and at this point it stands as is without major philosophical argument.

But the decision to look ahead seldom stems from rational persuasion. It will ever be a mystery to uninvolved researchers who pore through the record of the Mayflower company on the shores of the hostile new world, their number stricken to half by tragedy, that they greeted the spring with prayers of thanksgiving instead of wallowing in the fear of the next winter. What mysterious factor kept their hope alive? Or Washington at Valley Forge, Edison at Menlo Park after his thousandth failure, the American liberal in the face of the ineffectiveness of social idealism? There is no simple answer, but the assurance from memory and record that others have stuck to their helms and ridden out the storm is one helpful consideration. Indeed, the Bible offers us that.

If it were ever possible to match a past time with our own, we would be getting close to having demonstrable evidence for our justification of hope. That isn't going to be easy, as we live in a time as no other, with special circumstances no man has ever faced. How can we ever simulate a whole world facing imminent cancellation? How can we find another time when nations founded on the highest ideals of men couldn't seem to live their own dreams in justice and freedom from poverty? Was there ever a time when the greatest powers the world could amass neutralized each other in a contradictory paralysis so that an open sore like Vietnam might become the hemorrhage in which all human dignity bled to death?

No. There is no identical occasion in all history. Not in numbers or weaponry or potential horror or impotent knowledge or awesome technology. In sheer numbers of humans, tons of agony, acres of terror, instantaneous fright, the past at its loudest is only a feeble rustle of what we have to live with now. In the three atomic explosions of White Sands, Hiroshima, and Nagasaki, more firepower energy was released than in all the ordnance of World War II combined, and therein lies a picture. Nearly everything that takes place as the modern century avalanches on is in force or quantity or mass or importance the equal of the sum total of all history to that point.

But that is only true quantitatively. Man has always been man, and there are some characteristics having to do with love, hope, belief, faith, trust, fear, and failure that may wear different costumes and carry different weapons but inside stay very much the same. So to say that there has never been a time one could match with our own is only true in the external description. There *have* been times when the emotional context was similar. After all, whether it be an array of glistening spears or a nuclear bomber on the horizon one faces, fear is fear, and hope has to have the same reasons.

We may think we have greater reason for fear; we know very well the sky *can* fall. But in fact our despair is no deeper than a hundred other cultures have felt when a hostile army was coming over the hill, or imagination put a demon in every shadow. We may think that oblivion is more possible than it ever has been before, yet the Black Plague or the gas ovens of Buchenwald are facts of recorded history that we still can't fully believe.

So then, we look not so much at the measurements of the events of the past, but at their emotional content, and *voilà!* our day is not that new. This being true, the very fact that there even is an "our day" means that somebody survived what to him was the very worst, and thus that something from the way it happened to him in the past can speak with surprising relevance to us in the present.

In short, we can't match past and present and come up with a translated formula to cheer our sagging spirits; that sounds just a little bit like a sick kind of wishful thinking. But we can look back to some time when men felt as we feel, examine the symbols to which they clung, look beneath those symbols for some dynamic that can be honestly translated into our language, and we just *might* have something as important for us as the "Name one!" crowd has in withdrawal.

The Christian church, basically a community of stubborn insistence that there is more to man than meets the eye, has endured remarkable setbacks. Granted that each tragic time has left its purple scars, and that the church as we know it has been torn, decimated, compromised, and distorted so that it is far less at this moment than the world needs it to be. Yet, it *is*, and this even in spite of the fact that at its onset it only expected to endure for a generation before a universal day of judgment.

That first century of Christian history was a time of monumental disillusionment. There was the rejection by the Hebrew community, the parent fold. Almost immediately came the trauma of political and social opposition, and the climactic accusation of Nero that Christians were not only governmental security risks, but cannibals to boot. In addition, the new order of redeemed society and a visible Kingdom of God just didn't come about, and the dreary years dragged by, so that a whole reconsideration of the credibility of Christian promise had to be wearily undertaken.

As an almost-too-cruel-to-bear addition, the church itself developed flaws that brought keen disappointment to its most faithful adherents. Divisions, power struggles, heresies, condescensions to culture, cowardices, and petty rivalries brought a bitterness to the community that made many turn away in dismay.

One by one the first-generation Christians died or slipped away, and the church changed from being a community with a memory to being one centered in a relayed tradition, oral and written, and many opinions about the meaning of that tradition for life.

All the cards were stacked against the little flock, and by all rights they should have given up and blended into the scenery; it certainly would have been easier. But there was something in the nature of a survival attitude, a stubborn sense of meaning and destiny that seems to have been sufficiently widely held through oppressive times so that there is a church today. "In this period," writes Floyd V. Filson, "outward organizational expression of the unity of the Church was lacking. The Church generally sensed its unity. Those who shared the faith in the one basic gospel generally regarded themselves as members of one Church. But this unity was not expressed in outward form. . . . No discernible master plan knit their work together." (*A New Testament History,* p. 299; The Westminster Press, 1964.)

But we arrive at this point with only one, unexplainable but very demonstrable fact. The church exists. Why? In what ways were the first-century fathers able to make the emotional adjustments and find the necessary resources of morale and confirmation to get over that overwhelmingly crushing time? Whatever it was that they found just might be translatable into the language we speak and the thought forms we use.

It just might.

Since the canonical New Testament is made up of collated writings from the latter half of the first century, it is utterly dependable. It matters not what theory of authorship one holds about the Gospels and Epistles, their cities of origin or apostolic authenticity. The one fact of their antiquity means that they will reflect an unchallengeable validity about the tenor of the times. It is also rather certain that there is a diversity of viewpoints, a very wide latitude in the canon of ideas theological and impressions emotional. This again is an indicator of veracity. Even though there is much other ante-Nicene literature, I find that the spectrum of human affirmations found in the Scriptures can be transposed into a very wholesome diet for the contemporary mind. And the act of transposition need be no more than discovering the attitude corresponding to one's own, understanding a little of the New Testament context and its comparison to this one, and just letting go.

The New Testament abounds richly in allusions to the tough times. The Sermon on the Mount in Matthew, though an attempt to quote Jesus, was written in its current form over a generation later. Circumstances may have made the Evangelist's memory very selective. "Blessed are you," he quotes the Master, "when men shall revile you and persecute you and do all manner of evil against you in my name—for so persecuted they the prophets before you" (Matt. 5:11, 12). It takes no supersleuth detective work to see that behind those words must be considerable experience on the part of a community that has had to pay some kind of dear price to maintain its witness. "Blessed are those who are persecuted for righteousness' sake" (Matt. 5:10) is a way of saying to fellow members of the church wherever the Gospel is read that "we're all having a hard time of it, but there are more positive reasons to keep the faith than to give up."

The writings of Paul, or those letters which bear his authorship or influence, were actually written earlier than the Gospels and comprise the most original samples of early church life. Their greatest importance to our line of thought is the fact that they straddled the age of disenchantment in the church when the quick end of the world failed to materialize. "The end of all things is at hand" writes the author of I Peter (4:7), proceeding with a teaching on how to hold fast with loving patience. But he has lived long enough to feel the cold reality in the winter of waiting, for he later talks of a "fiery ordeal . . . as though something strange were happening" (4:12) and concludes this passage with the admonition to those who suffer to "do right and entrust their souls to a faithful Creator" (4:19).

This was indeed a difficult and most confusing time. Jesus' teachings had led the early Christians to feel very expectant, and the subsequent sayings of the apostles had quickened their trust that God would right the oppressive, unfair, unjust disorderliness of the world in a mighty blow. Each new day dawning untroubled by the heavenly lightning proved a frustrating and demoralizing experience for the church under duress. And when local and world history began to deal the church a series of urgent crises, it was understandable for churchmen to cry out in bewilderment: "Where is the promise of his coming? For ever since the fathers feel asleep, all things have continued as they were from the beginning of creation" (II Peter 3:4).

Paul has left enough of himself in those writings and impressions which are preserved in the canon for us to see a remarkable enduring pastoral concern as the call bears more and more upon him to explain the unexplainable. To the Thessalonian church he renders a beautiful and tender assurance: "In all our distress and affliction we have been comforted about you through your faith . . . , praying earnestly night and day that we may see you face to face and supply what is lacking in your faith" (I Thess. 3:7, 10). It seems apparent that even at the writing of these words Paul himself was still clinging to the imminent hope, yet seeing with great insight the possibility of a continuing world and an extended time of tribulation for the church. One can only, after giving honest assessment to the pressures and frustrations of such a time, give due respect to a persistent community and a strong leader.

As the early church seems to shrug its shoulders and settle down for a more permanent residence in this world, one can see through the wide cracks left by the unpretentious writings of the day, both accommodation in disappointment, and wistful courage. Ignatius of Antioch, an early Christian leader who may even have been successor to Paul as chief apostle of Asia Minor, fortunately left his record in a surviving series of letters, some to the churches in Philadelphia and Smyrna, and to his friend Polycarp. Ignatius was seized in 107 by Pliny, an adviser to Trajan, and taken to Rome to be martyred as public entertainment. There is no doubt that his dedication to his faith made it a privilege for him to give his life in witness, and his martyrdom may have been a pacesetter for the unnumbered others who paid the same price.

But after having described the darkness, the lonely suffering, and the childish, unrealistic naïveté of dying for an apparently defenseless and impotent cause, one has to stand back and admit something else. It was during this time that a vision of a this-world-belongingness took deep root and the scope of the church spread like dandelion seeds before the wind. Kenneth Scott Latourette comments that the church began its third century as a definitely "universalist, international, inter-dependent" fellowship, with a worldwide and deeply human outlook.

This story fascinates me, not only because it is truth demonstrable beyond the Christian bias, but because I can't help looking at these days, with their frightening power conflicts and monumental inhumane injustices, their frustrating roadblocks to conscience and their inability to promise anything at all bright about tomorrow, with irrepressible, excited hope. No, we haven't suffered at all as the early Christians did, in the way they did. But we are undergoing a tortuous and ever so subtle agony of the spirit in our inability to interpret the times in accord with our idea of God, or good, or the worth of virtue. In that we can look at the imbalance of privilege only with enormous sensations of guilt, and at our churches only with a heart-hurting wonder at their provinciality, we may even be suffering a deeper and more demonic persecution. The early churchmen at least saw the sharp line between holding fast and giving up, and knew why they did what they did, but in our day there is such a vast blob of ambiguity about whether we're in or we're out that even in the heart of the church there is a transient loneliness.

Strangely enough, we are asking the same questions of ourselves that the New Testament, and especially the book of Revelation, seeks to answer. Our times may be different, but our fallible little human hearts are very much the same. We may have had nearly twenty centuries' more experience at the Christian life, but when our backs are against that cold stone wall, we cry for the very same assurances, spit out the same kinds of resentments, and find it easy to have the same general cynicisms.

If you can call the apostolic affirmations of the Scriptures and early centuries good words, and evidently they were, then it's time for more. Or perhaps it's time for the same ones revisited.

2

The Church Is Inadequate for Today

Both disillusionment and cynicism abound as characteristic attitudes toward the Christian church. Perhaps the most pathos is to be seen in the way those outside the church react with sadness or violence to its failures. Evidently they assume that the religious community represents itself to the world as being without flaw, and that its continuation persists in the illusion. It's not just that the church is a hypocritical sham that bothers them; it's that it *could* be and by all rights *should* be effecting its teaching of love and healing.

The church's divisions and sectarian rivalries don't just dismay the watching audience. They become actually incensed; it's an irksome, angering thing to see grown people play with sacred possibilities. No wonder Bertrand Russell said it was the church, not the Jews, that killed Christ! Gandhi's well-known statement is familiar to most college students: "The main reason I am not a Christian is the unchristianity of the Christian Church." Sammy Davis, Jr., raised in the Protestant tradition, converted to Judaism as a protest to the church's inconsistency on the color line.

They have a point. The dynamic is not unlike the antagonism so many feel against the police, or the mayor, or the high school principal. These figures are symbols of total benevolence, and the purity of the myth is as easily contaminated by the tiniest spot as the surgeon's hands between the washbasin and the operating room. And the pollution, little as it is, ruins the whole value of desired infallibility. The church has *no right* to be imperfect—it simply isn't entitled to that luxury; the world needs it too much. So if there is any indication of its being less than it's supposed to be, that's proof that the whole shebang is impossible, the claims to God's purity downright mistaken, and we sinners aren't so damned bad after all! The life of Joseph Stalin is here a condensed pattern of much of modern thought. Committed early in life to the priesthood, a student in a theological seminary, he became adamantly bitter at the moral decay and narrowness of vision of the Russian Church. That he then devoted his life to another kind of means to bring a new order shows how deeply motivated he was to belong to a movement of meaning.

This outsider's scorn has marked every decade of the last hundred years, in different forms. Robert G. Ingersoll added splashes of rich color to the last part of the nineteenth century, and Clarence Darrow made the most of it in the early twentieth. College campuses and syndicated newspaper columns became the sound chambers of venomous ventilation. Bull sessions in the barracks and patter in the parlor resounded with it. That it all had undertones of wishing it were otherwise is made obvious by reactions under stress. World War II brought a pious silence over the scorners; there were reported to be "no atheists in foxholes"; and during the Battle of Stalingrad the Russian Church suddenly became legal. All of which indicates that no matter how loud we talk when our position is safe, we still need our totems in the dark.

The dominant tone is that of disappointment in what might have been but isn't. The rejected lover is angered and hurt; the dreamer becomes sarcastic; and the optimistic do-gooder groans, "What the hell?" In this modern time, when our technology makes all the fantasies of the Brothers Grimm seem ordinary and the caliph's flying carpet antiquated, when the laser beam can dissolve space, matter, and time, why the hell can't the church get off its duff? Why do we still have corruption in government, riots in the cities, crime on the ascendancy, assassinations of good leaders, and the same cringing fears, pains, ulcers, and loneliness that we always did? Why is the church still building huge little-used barns on the corners of our streets and chasing that almighty dollar when there are so unbelievably many poor? It just doesn't make any sense at all. It seems that the church just may be analogous to a group of doctors during an epidemic who, with their cupboards well stocked with the healing serum, are paralyzed by infighting over what size hypodermic needle to use, and merely motion to the frantic public to pick up a band-aid by the door and be sure to leave a generous donation.

If it's any comfort, which it may not be to the cynical, 'twas ever thus. There is ample testimony in the New Testament that the first-century world gave the same cynical back-of-the-hand. Jesus ran into it in his own hometown and eventually became its victim on the cross. The disciples accepted it as the order of the day wherever they went, and the very existence of the church anywhere was always one of operation in contention.

Not only that, it *ought* to be so. The world at large has every right to look on the church with a hurt sneer, because the church does represent a fragmented and soiled reflection of the holy. The very exasperation that all non-Christians display is a confession of faith that man responds to the all-absorbing dream of purity. The measure of his dismay or scorn is the same disappointment anyone would have at having the bus splash mud all over your party clothes as it pulls to a stop to take you to the party! The anger comes because a better development was anticipated, and it could so nearly have been.

One could go on and on about those who have felt threatened or accused or insecure because of the gospel. As one analysis of today's right-wing extremists goes, it's those who have the most to lose by change of any kind who are resisting hysterically change of every kind. This line of thought would move on to the prize observation that everybody who throws mud at the church or any symbol of human concern is himself in neurotic trouble. It's possibly true, but it amounts in a way to saying the same thing about non-Christians that we've already said, namely, that they've got a problem of feeling deep needs, overexpecting, and have a large residue of disappointed hostility. The church has no business writing its problems off as the sickness of others; it's too sick itself to be accusatory. Besides, it's in the business, according to the fourth chapter of Luke, of being on the sick people's side in the battle for healing, not against them.

So if the nonchurch world cares to throw a few stones as indications of justifiable disappointment and occasionally inflict a major wound on the body of the church, Christians should acknowledge the compliment, feel needed and desperately wanted, and with genuine honesty "pray for them that despitefully use you" (Luke 6:28). Evidently the apostles did just that, not as a dreary burden, but as a holy calling.

Running away from its enemies and discrediting its critics were *not* marks of the church that lived through the early storms. In the cries of derision, or anger, or accusation, the church both proclaimed its faith and heard the accents of disguised calls for help. Rather than yielding to the temptation to tell the hostile world to go to hell, the church eventually found its meaning in sharing the hell of the world in both suffering and hope, hurt by its own imperfections, but revelling in the forgiveness of a God who showed he knew what it was all about by being hurt too.

By all odds, the most important kind of criticism of the church is that which comes from inside. Though they who stand outside may be articulate, incisive, and deadly in their accusations, and correct in their indictments, there is a cutoff point in their effectiveness. They are describing a community whose main characteristic is that of a loyalty involvement, and their very noninvolvement is the main factor that keeps them from saying the word most needed, most deeply cutting.

We are now a part of an international scene in which some nations, such as the People's Republic of China and the Republic of South Africa, are playing roles we can neither understand nor find ways to accept. Our distance gives us a certain helpful perspective in analyzing and criticizing that makes our words of historical and political importance. But when such a country comes to that time of decision, or confession, or description which brings its whole national life under the scrutiny of those who pay the price of being there, our contribution is minimal.

So it is that the John Q. Agnostics, the Jewish and Muslim brothers, and the whole host of those who can see the cracks in the walls so clearly from the surrounding landscape, abrasively stimulating as they are, can only introduce the subject of the church's failings by saying the obvious, and at that point their contribution is complete. From then on it is those within, the Augustines, Aquinases, Husses, Savonarolas, Luthers, Pope Johns, and Harvey Coxes, who must take over and have the full sway of their particularly equipped viewpoints and their loving agitation. As a matter of fact, the voices within have always said the most devastating, the most deeply disapproving, the most bitingly critical things. Anyone who wanted documented evidence to completely discredit the church would find more than ample ammunition for his campaign in the writings and teachings of its own loving and deeply loyal leaders in every generation!

Some of us will be surprised to discover that the restless inner voice of discontent within the church dates from apostolic times. There is the tendency to think it is only typical of this presumptuous, blatantly frank twentieth century, and that the usual order of the past was one of mute acceptance. If the New Testament is a correct reflection of how the church got under way, its repeated instances of self-disappointment and inner dissension should assure anyone that a monolithic community it never was. Nor that it has been made up of or led by a cadre of simplistic virtue peddlers. Their hopes that the church could be historically effective were even higher than those of the magic-seeking populace, and thus their disappointment greater.

It's all there in the New Testament record and in the noncanonical literature and in the writings of non-Christian historians such as Josephus and even Pliny the Younger, who persuaded Emperor Trajan to maintain his antichristian policy. We see the neophyte evangelist Paul opposing Peter to his face at Jerusalem, eventually bringing about a major hearing of the church leadership to determine attitudes toward the Jewish tradition, a subject about which there were many strong feelings.

All this is by way of saying to those who are distressed about the wave of antichurch feeling found everywhere today that it's always been, and is somewhat justifiable. And to those within the church who are dismayed or hurt by hearing their own leaders and colleagues speak with criticism, or disapproval, or even bitterness, about the very household in which so many of us find shelter, again let it be said that the church has always been a matter of expressed disappointment to those who love it most.

The final book of the New Testament is an amazing work, and that not just because of its elaborate imagery. It is a document dedicated to the picking up of the sagging Christian spirit in a dreary time, a definite word of assurance and hope to a community seemingly overwhelmed by impossible odds. I took it in hand after the incidents already described to catch a bit of the flavor of what the mysterious "John of Patmos" had to say to another time of despair. Whoever he was, and nobody seems to know much about him, he seemed to have enough Christian stature on his own and prestige across the church so that what he said really meant something. His code is not at all unbreakable, just the language of other well-known apocalyptic literature, and most of his audience knew the Jewish house-language of dreams and visions well enough to follow him closely. At any rate, the first very impressive surprise is that the book of Revelation starts off exactly where the armchair groaners, the incisive Harvey Coxes and Peter Bergers, the threatened conservatives of our day, start, namely, criticizing the church as being inadequate!

Many of the allusions in the first three chapters of Revelation are beyond us. They are passing historical references that are details lost in the shuffling of the centuries.

To equate them straight across the board to the problems of today would be something less than intelligent, for the whole scene has changed a thousand times over. But because, as we have already noted, there is a similarity in the emotional atmosphere then and now, and the New Testament writings were directed more at the morale than the method, we can look here at the old list of churchly ills, marveling that there is also a new list, which can be recounted in the same hopeful ways. And in listing the new as we name over the old, we feel that the voice of assurance that pulled them through just might have a similar encouragement to put our day in perspective of promise.

So the book of Revelation begins with a list of seven judgments on the church of the first century. Seven kinds of sickness, seven reasons why the little community to whom Jesus had said, "Fear not, little flock, for it is your Father's good pleasure to give you the kingdom" (Luke 12:32), hadn't been up to the heritage.

And in my mind's eye there immediately appeared a new list of seven. I didn't have to conjure them up from a strained imagination; they were handed to me quickly and openly by the leadership of the church of today. Perhaps in the recounting of them we can begin the same process of hearing God's promises and singing doxologies that the Apocalypse leads to.

The First Crisis: Institutionalism
To the church at Ephesus write: "You have given up loving each other as you did at first." (Rev. 2:1, 4.)

Theoretically, the church is a community founded upon the voluntary interpersonal values of love, respect, and service, the very things that can never be depersonalized or formalized. Yet the church is an organization which, from the time the first apostles met together to do systematic planning, began to systematize the curiously unsystematic and formalize the preciously informal. None but the most childish among us would ever say that the church can survive on an intuitive atmosphere of irresponsible nonstructuring, yet all of us vary only by degree in our resentment toward the institutional coldness it seems to us the church has attained.

It takes a real, special determination of faith to behold the enormous effort and energy going into the committee and administrative machinery of a medium-sized local parish church and to trust that the compassion and joy of the gospel has its principal expression here. What may be the classic lament of the modern psalmist is sung in every part of the land: "I went to that church seeking help and understanding, and the only time they ever come to see me is to ask for money."

Modern Protestantism is still coasting on its own unresolved assumption that its protest against the deadly corrosives of overinstitutionalism, political establishment, and undeserved earthly power could be justified by erecting a system of its own that carries along the germs of the same infection. The practices of owning land and building edifices and hiring professional staff never really came up for an in-depth theological review, for they were the only way the spirit could keep from being disembodied. Even though the so-called Reformed tradition would be the first to loudly deny it, any institutionalism becomes self-defensive and soon develops an apologetic that transcends both doctrine and basic good sense. After all, we do live in the time of Parkinson and his laws.

On the theory that one is far more willing to sacrifice if he has little to lose, small groups such as the Religious Society of Friends and service wings such as the Salvation Army have maintained a stubborn simplicity and a disciplined program of putting out everything that comes in. But this doesn't accurately describe either the main-line standard-brand churches of East and West or even most of the splinter sects that tried to reclaim the freedom of voluntariness. An overnight camp can become a winter embankment, which of necessity has to become a fort. And forts become cities, with highly developed programs of self-protection, survival, and perpetual residence.

All of this is a matter of dismay to those who long to recapture the spirit of the primitive church, a pilgrim community not taught to think of itself as needing justification, but existing around a function of proclaiming startlingly good news, restoring the broken fragments of mankind, and setting an atmosphere of gratitude and expectation. If there were any way to measure the ergons of energy, the man-hours of time, and the emotional juice poured into the institutional church in comparison with the actual effect in human warmth, released compassion, and history-changing social good, the final score, many suspect, would make a Rube Goldberg machine look like a modern jet plane.

It was probably in the aftermath of this kind of guilt twinge that the Episcopal Bishop of New York announced to the world that the gigantic Cathedral of St. John the Divine, sitting as it does on the edge of Harlem, overlooking one of America's greatest concentrations of human misery, would stand unfinished as a symbol of identification with the poor. In one sense it was a majestic gesture, a symbol of genuine relatedness between cold stone and hurting hearts. In another sense, it was a confession to the world that this very institutional crisis troubled and stayed and even shamed the whole church from pew to hierarchy. It cast the shadow of uncleanliness upon the whole superstructure, mutely accepting the indictment that the church in material is something less than the church in spirit.

Even Pope Paul VI gets into this act. By selling off a jeweled crown and giving to the poor, he made a penitential bow in the direction of the embarrassed necessity, and his servant Bishop Fulton J. Sheen, of Rochester, chose Ash Wednesday to make an outright gift to the city of—of all things—a whole parish church and its half-acre of valuable urban dirt. But deadly institutionalism won the next round in that one, and a red-faced bishop had to take the gift back when he found it "ecclesiastically inadvisable" to go through with it. An institution *can* at least try to be human, after all.

What is affectionately called the "American ideal" carries with it a strain of individuality, stubbornly affirmed as being above and more important than any freedom-killing arrangement men can make. Just give a man a plow and forty acres, and let him market, teach, worship, express his civic responsibilities, any way he wants to. This subjectivity, in which the "good feelings" of the person come first, well-nigh threatened to wrest the rural and small-town church from its connectional witness and make it into an island of American folk ritual. True, it carried a strong oral tradition of remotely Biblical Calvinistic overtones, but no kind of written or institutional authority went unresented. The ultimate validation of any idea or belief was the great Protestant sentence starter, "It seems to me . . ." or just "I think . . ."

All of which is just another side of the coin of anti-institutionalism. And it may well be that this feeling of individualism, rather than being an expression of an ideal, is really a reaction stimulated by crisis and nurtured in fear. Institutions, after all, are the inventions of men erecting scaffolds upon the sites where they have to build their collective services. Institutions develop as the result of dreams, insights, discoveries, social developments, and societal success. And once an institution is under way, those who worked to organize it give a great sigh of relief that what they couldn't bring about so well by themselves is now a hope with real possibilities.

This is the way it was in the early church. It wasn't that the early Christians set out to draw up a constitution and bylaws and elect officers; it was rather that they had a purpose and soon found themselves reaching in all directions for ways to fulfill it. So far, so good. It would be very simple to say that institutionalism is thoroughly defendable and anyone who doesn't like it simply doesn't understand the hard necessities of organized life. And it makes a lot of sense—the church institutionalized to the glory of God!

But that doesn't really answer everything, or even some of the most bewildering dilemmas of history. It doesn't give much of an explanation to the European Jews who for centuries underwent vast indignities at the hands of an institution that was proclaiming compassion for all men. It leaves a major question mark on the record of religious man in reference to the mysterious silence from both Rome and Geneva while millions of "non-Aryans" were being done away with in mass genocide. It doesn't add up that an institution that not only owns major landholdings but controls amazing human resources has never really called a universal emergency on the awesome dehumanization of world power politics, poverty, racial injustice, but has continued to stress in its program and promotion the primacy of devotion and giving—to the church.

One can only wonder if the crisis is any worse now than

it was in the first century. Of course, by volume there is no comparison. But in the depth of the disillusionment, the dampening of the enthusiasm and all-out commitment of those who put so much of their life hope in the movement that had so much promise, there is an abiding poignancy in the words, "You have given up loving each other as you did at first." Since there was such a fragility and inexperienced innocence about those early Christians, there must be a major insight in just reflecting on the fact that the church prevailed where the Roman Empire died.

Each of the sections of the Apocalypse that exposes the critical flaws in the church of that day appends a cryptic remark: "Let he who has an ear listen to what the Spirit says to the churches" (Rev. 2:7). In this case, these words follow a dry observance that God isn't eternally committed to any structure, and that to him institutions can be changed like a flat tire. If the church as an institution doesn't shape up, "I will come to you quickly and remove your lampstand" (Rev. 2:5). We're going to miss you around here. Bad as the church is, it can shape up to the situation. If it doesn't, the Spirit will find another vehicle. Institutions are not indispensable.

That's what it says. Right in the second chapter of the book of Revelation, a writing fully intended to strengthen the failing spirits of Christians in crisis. The gospel and the human values it exalts are more important than any container they happen to be shipped in. That's the word of hope. The church can be better. Even more, it can be replaced. Now get on with your job of using the tools you have to proclaim the gospel. The world can't get along without it. Let all the irksome disappointments be voiced and heard; let us all chafe under the imperfection of this corrupt and inefficient human world. Evidently there is no way open to us that is safe from being misused

44

and damaging personhood. So, let us make do with what we have. The ultimate result is God's problem; faithfulness to this minute and its ministry is ours.

The common, ordinary automobile engine is a symbol of institutionalism. Its inefficiency is appalling to those sophisticated engineers who really know the facts. There is far more latent energy in a gallon of gasoline than any engine ever built can get—perhaps five times as much. Imagine! If one considers twenty miles to the gallon to be good mileage, just consider that if the engine were really up to snuff, it would be more like a hundred! But inefficiency is part of the reality; there's no choice but to take what we can get. The major part of the push is passed off in heat and waste.

Yet we insist on using the auto. By the millions, yet! Wasteful as it is, it still delivers *some* power. It works, in its poor way. Rant and rave as we will, disclaim the unreasonable and shameful misuse of valuable resources as loud as we can, we still wind up by using the car and its internal-combustion engine because it's the best arrangement yet.

That's institutionalism.

The church has immense responsibilities to fulfill, in the lifting of the human spirit and its ideals, the practice of justice and love. "Let anyone who has an ear listen to what the Spirit says to the churches."

The Second Crisis: Technology
To the church at Smyrna write: "I know your tribulation and your poverty—but you are rich." (Rev. 2:8, 9.)

The whole concept of the church as a religious community is deeply rooted in many centuries of an agrarian society. Nothing stood between man and the awesome, limitless sky, survival was the result of expending muscle on the land, and communication depended on the raised voice. People were born, raised, educated, and used up in the same location. Communities were natural gatherings of people who had geography and family ties in common. The whole "theology" of the congregation as a gathered society has all its assumptions in ancient or at best medieval contexts. Some parts of Christianity haven't even divested themselves of the pre-Ptolemaic cosmology with its picture of the firmament—water, that is—encircling heaven and earth and the lower realms. Most of those who have are still dangling in the Copernican wilderness with little insight into the impact of Einstein on all thought.

It was no less a contemporary leader of religious thought than Nikita Khrushchev who delivered one of the insights of the century. It followed the history-making flight of Sputnik I, the first man-made vessel to send back signals from outer space. "See," said the Soviet premier, "that proves there is no God. Christianity has always taught that God is up in heaven, and Sputnik went up there and saw no God." One has to take this remark very seriously, for it reflects the kind of simplistic and limited faith the Communist world thinks it is denying. Evidently the vast multitudes of Russians through the years conceptualized a deity who just wouldn't stand up under scientific scrutiny, and the modern age had no trouble at all knocking that one down.

It probably does no good at all to observe that if that is the kind of God the Russians don't believe in, it is also the kind of God the contemporary church doesn't believe in. But it would be a hard go to convince the Communists of that, as they would find it hard to believe that we disbelieve what they believe we believe. And it's all pretty well our fault anyway for perpetuating our mythology in its ancient terminology without upgrading it, as it should be upgraded, with the terms and reference frameworks of secular thought.

To illustrate: The Bible was written in a day when the "whole world" was the eastern end of the Mediterranean Sea; no one had the experience or imagination to see God stretching himself much farther. Now we are talking about the possibility of discovering other forms of intelligent life on other planets in the galaxy. To those whose religion is too literally in Old Testament terms there is the problem of either accepting that there could be other worlds with their own gods, or going through the painful process of developing an infinite God. Had we woven into our preaching and theology, as we should have, the ballooning dimensions of reality from horizon to Orion to infinity, this ridiculous conversation wouldn't have had to exist.

But it does exist, and on other more subtle planes. In a day when it doesn't take physical presence to have intimate communication, the church yet persists in thinking of itself in terms of gathering for worship and interaction. In a world where instantaneous intercontinental conversation is becoming more common, the church still thinks of national and regional traditions as being too precious to tamper with. In a day of increasing mobility, as in the U.S. where families move every five years, we Christians still talk of a parish as being a stable, continuing unit, ministering its ordinances to birth, life, and death on a single continuum.

The crisis is simply that something very profound is happening to humanity, its self-identification, its consciousness of life and movement, that is not reflected very clearly in the church. And since the church is supposed to be rooted in the very depths of the human spirit where whatever most matters dwells, those who look for the church to know what's going on are disappointed. Saint Patrick's Cathedral in New York City is the symbol of this. Once, those Gothic twin towers presided over the mid-town district, proudly and reverently pointing heavenward and dominating the sky and the concepts of men. Now, dwarfed by the gigantic buildings of Rockefeller Center, thrown into shadow for most of the day, the church stands almost as a museum piece of the way things used to be but aren't any more, for men are more impressed by the high rise of their own technology than by how God was seen a century ago. Stalin's famous snort, "How many legions does the pope have?" is echoed by the modern intellectual who says that science has dissipated the mystery of religion by its prolongation of life, transplantation of organs, test-tube conception, sterility pills, emotion-controlling drugs, and revealing of the unknowns in outer space.

Arend van Leeuwen, theologian and student of Oriental languages, claims that the changes in our time are so profound that we are living in a completely unexplored and unexperienced human environment, "in which the unity of knowledge, the order of society, the order of ideas, the very notions of society and culture, have changed and will not return to what they have been in the past." The World Conference on Church and Society that met in Geneva in 1966 proclaimed that "incredibly rapid technological change is one of the main characteristics of society today. A new kind of world is being created by it, one that presents man with unprecedented power and freedom while confronting him at the same time with equally unprecedented problems (*Christians in the Technical and Social Revolutions of Our Time*).

And of course we can't overlook Marshall McLuhan's piercing reflections on what the miracle of instantaneous communications does to the human personality. He compares the new electronic media to man's central nervous system, which is now technologically extended into a "global embrace, abolishing both space and time as far as our planet is concerned" (*Understanding Media: The Extensions of Man,* p. 3; McGraw-Hill Book Company, Inc., 1965).

This is a formidable problem. No matter how loyally our contemporary churchman pooh-poohs the disclaimers, even he is a creature of modern times, and just to stay with the church, he finds it necessary to do very fancy philosophical footwork to keep his integrity. The long discussions that used to prevail on Sunday evenings over the problem of faith and evolution were just the opening fanfares to the agonized wrestlings. Hear, for instance, a voice from *within* the church, a former president of the Society for the Scientific Study of Religion. "In a surprise-free world," says Peter Berger, "I see no reversal of the process of secularization produced by the industrialization." In a speech at The New School for Social Research, where he teaches, Mr. Berger (as reported in *The New York Times,* Feb. 25, 1968) commented, "I think people will become so bored with what religious groups have to offer that they will look elsewhere."

We don't know, of course, how things were with the church at Smyrna or anywhere in A.D. 96, but it is apparent that there was serious trouble. The Christians were being ridiculed and slandered by some group who evidently saw no authenticity or possibility in their movement. To them comes, in this old but wise writing, the admonition to "be faithful unto death" (Rev. 2:10). Where that meant persecution and martyrdom to the early Christians, in these days it may mean more the death of keeping abreast of a marvelously advancing world and yet, in faith, keeping ahead of it.

Established religion tends to be conservative, that is, resist any kind of news that changes the dimensions of the universe. Every new development in modern science has brought an anguished cry from the household of faith as though God himself had been threatened with a conspiracy to render him obsolete. The Amish of Pennsylvania, trotting down the country roads in their horse-drawn broughams, symbolize the weariness that besets so many of us when the pace of just keeping up with the world and still feeling the acceptance of a personal God becomes too much. Fortunately, there are still some who can live in a moving world and see the relevance of the gospel without being threatened because the landscape is forever changing.

"Let anyone who has an ear listen." There is a monstrous presumptuousness in trusting that the mind of man will ever encompass the universe. Much is yet to come; perhaps we have yet unveiled only one thousandth of the discoveries and advances the physical world offers us. It is just as meaningful for me, in the light of both the historical faith and the exciting pace of the pursuit of knowledge today, to feel that we are on the threshold of a technology that will fling the skies open like cosmic gates, and to be expectantly and trustingly happy about it, as it is to follow Berger's pessimism. To those well read in the ways in which the human mind adjusts, there is as much a miracle in the ice-pack cracking of Vatican II as in the laser beam. So, in the new world, the church will have new forms. We will have enlarged, modified, technicolored, stereophonic concepts of the God we first knew in black and white. So we have to change. So?

Technology may indeed change the living contexts and modify all the sensations of living. It may completely revise the standpoint from which humanity views the world. It may throw into complete obsolescence the entire methodology of the church in liturgy, social service, pastoral care. But there are some basic givens about being creatures that will always need the ministry of interpersonal dignity and cosmic belonging. We don't know what they are. At this juncture, we don't need to know. Just trust that Reality, whatever that is, has a quality of enduring tolerance for human life, and "be faithful." It's all a matter of what frightens us, and in the long run, those things frighten us that we imagine to be demonic, and those things inspire us that we treat expectantly. It is so with technology.

The Third Crisis: Confession and Liturgy

And to the church at Pergamum write: "You dwell where Satan sits, yet you adhere to my name, you have not renounced." (Rev. 2:12, 13.)

For a church that started off enjoying being together, and feeling a sacramental importance in eating together, and being truly liberated to be our natural selves when relating to one another within the fellowship, we certainly have screwed up the works. We have taken careful and responsible pains to describe precisely what happens when we congregate, and thereby have confounded the issue. Different ones saw different things, and when we wrote out the richness of our diversity we found to our embarrassment that we were contradicting one another.

To a communicant of the Eastern Orthodox family, worship is a community experience of the classic timelessness and spacelessness of God and Mother Church. That part of self that is spoken to in the Divine Liturgy is partially removed from reality in an almost hallucinatory ecstasy of belonging to a community of infinite dimension, presided over by a Christ beyond humanity, implanted over and above in an endless act of blessing and warmth. Reason? Description? Intellect? Theology? Are you kidding? It's not what *happens* in the Old Slavonic chants, it's what *is*, and let the circumstances of the outside world go hang. In here, with the air full of incense and Holy Presence, the ear blessed with the sacred words in song, the eye ministered to by gilded icons, this is a taste of heaven, another world.

Western Christianity has wound itself up into knots over trying to keep the Eucharist authentic and has developed some of the most ridiculous prohibitions in all history. Is Christ *in*, or *of*, or *represented by* the sacramental elements? Is Almighty God bound by the priestly enactments? Most of the world stands by in incredulous indifference. It is indeed, as the Apocalypse tells of ancient Pergamum, the wielding of a sharp sword with a double edge.

This isn't limited to the acts of worship of the church, but extends to all its interior relationships. Just who are we when we come together, anyway, and what is the significance of thinking we are in the presence of God? And isn't he everywhere else anyway? If going to church is some kind of virtue, what will be the morality of being together by technology, as through TV or taped replay of sensuous experiences?

When five thousand people crowded into a big-city cathedral recently to hear a Mass sung by, of all people, Duke Ellington and his merry men, there were more theoretical questions raised than notes in the scale. Was this an authentic representation of an updated church at wor-

ship? Was it a forced novelty to persuade the rapidly dis-
interested that the church was worth getting interested in
again? Was it an invasion of the specially notable and
separate atmosphere of the church by the vulgar capri-
ciousness of the lighthearted and uninvolved irreverent?
Was it anything more than a concert of the new in the
setting of the old?

Probably the appearance of guitars in the Evangelical
Church of Mexico, of smiles on the faces of worshipers
in Amsterdam, and the mouthing of current slang in the
pulpit by preachers in Milwaukee are much more genuine signs of breakthrough in this crisis. But they are all
bellwethers, and more noteworthy because of their rarity
than anything else.

To come right down to it, the church of today is downright embarrassed about the meaning of being gathered
for anything at all. Which probably reflects a deeper awk-
wardness about being a church anyway in a world that
doesn't know what to do with it. Yet, in spite of the loose-
ness of it all, the church insists on continuing in all its
clumsiness as the community of The Drama. Nobody
knows how in the world it can ever be captured so that
we feel good about it, but it is this arena in which we are
made most aware of the intersection of the cyclic monot-
ony of birth-life-death with a Drama that unfolds itself in
both Truth and Deeds.

It is our insecurity that makes us hang up all the time
and makes us cling to the visible nonessentials; it is the
underlying validity we cannot deny that compels us to
keep at it. In the now barren cathedral in Cuernavaca,
Mexico, marimbas appear before the altar, white-shirted
mariachi troubadors cry out to a bongo beat, *"¡Señor, ten
piedad de nosotros!"* (Lord, have mercy upon us!), and
worshipers there and listeners from afar know down deep

that it is a universal and very, very human cry. The minute we try to explain how it is that men never really feel that mercy granted, we have dismantled the whole effect. Yet, spines tingle, flesh quivers, men make decisions and commitments, and society feels the effect of an outward-turned compassion.

It is the problem of twentieth-century man that he *thinks*. He thinks too damned much. He thinks that every occasion is subject to analysis and every relationship has its rationale. He thinks that the nobility of love and the beauty of interpersonal devotion can be programmed into some mysterious computer and be printed out in block letters. So he looks at the church in its common acts and asks precisely the most improper question, "What's happening, and what does it mean?" The Lord's Table then becomes a spread of bread crumbs and grape juice, of ritual and habit, of frozen faces and forced silence.

Behold the Civic Center plaza in downtown Chicago, and put yourself there in your imagination on a sunny August afternoon in 1967, at the magic moment. A special gift in the form of a huge piece of sculpture had been designed for the city by none other than Pablo Picasso himself, and now the time had come for its long-awaited unveiling. Down came the blue shroud, to be followed by silence, then laughter, then applause, and from then and on and on, questions. I stood in that plaza for two hours on a Saturday evening watching the hundreds who came to stand and gawk and talk. It goes without saying that the reactions and theories and opinions were of all kinds and on all levels. But everybody who came was affected in some way and went away somewhat changed from the way he came.

The prize observation to make, however, is that to the thousands who asked, pushed, shouted, and wept the question "What does it mean?" Picasso makes *absolutely no reply*. The work of art stands above words, it transcends any kind of interpretation. It speaks to every beholder in a particularly unique way and depth, and any description of it would immediately vitiate its beauty for the 99 percent who hadn't seen it that way. Picasso, then, is not only a genius as an artist but an extraordinarily wise man. Had the church only been that perceptive with the Lord's Table, offering it as its own teaching, ministering to all kinds of men, for to all of us bread is the most profound of symbols!

There was undoubtedly this kind of crisis in the first century. When Paul (or whoever it was) set out to instruct the Corinthian church about conduct at the table, he expended not one useless syllable on the doctrine of the thing. He just said, "Do it!" and keep your life open to the doing of it. Can you imagine the teen-agers of our day, or any day, enthralled at the growth of their own gonads, needing to be talked into a kiss? Do you know anyone who has to have the theology, dynamics, doctrine, and rationale of kissing explained to him before he can give himself permission to try it? Put a virile young man next to an affectionate, luscious young lady in the front seat of a convertible parked on a high cliff and ask him to analyze the bacteriology of lips in contact, and you've killed it, brother, you've killed it.

For what happens when Christians come together is one of those gestures that speaks thousands of words beyond words, like a pat on the back, the squeeze of a hand, the approving nod in a lonely world. What more needs to be said than *that's what it is!* The church lives because people say something to each other in their recognizing each other that transcends the threatening and the embarrassment and doesn't try to explain a thing.

Precisely the same is true of creedal confessions. There is a remarkable beauty about a confession that appears in the line of years as a milestone. "Hey, look! Here's what we've discovered!" There is a deadly morbidity about a confession that is used as a measuring instrument or a membership requirement. To spring to one's feet in church and recite the Apostles' Creed or sing the Nicene Creed or read together portions of some historic confession is to me the same kind of emotional experience as whispering to the woman in my arms, "I love you," or expressing my irrepressible admiration or gratitude to a friend. The doing of it is a genuine release of accumulated powerful positive convictions. But to require that another brother Christian use the same way, and to suspect him of unorthodoxy if he can't, is the fly in the ointment of the whole confessional system. I remember seeing a woman dragging a ten-year-old boy into a carnival, screaming at him, "I brought you all the way here to have a good time, and you're going to have fun if I have to beat you black and blue!"

Confessions are precious, beautiful little sparkling moments in the unfolding of the church, and should be cherished as pictures in the family album. But when they become frozen in solid concrete as the definitive footprints of the Holy Spirit, and that's the authoritative shape and size of his foot, we've got problems. The crisis is that we can't keep from confessing, nor should we. And yet we've got to keep our orientation ahead, not back. Let him who has ears hear.

The Fourth Crisis: Theology
And to the church at Thyatira write: "You are doing more than you did at first—still you are tolerating Jezebel." (Rev. 2:18, 19, 20.)

There is a quizzical irony in the fact that theology, once called "Queen of the Sciences," serves both to unite and to divide the church. The early centuries saw a succession of doctrinal disputes and conciliar decisions that produced the ecumenical creeds. After each such decision came a housecleaning of all heretics, a purification of the faithful, and the creed became more an instrument of measuring orthodoxy than a channel of liberating the adoring spirit. Some centuries stand out as the peaks of theological advance because of certain men or movements that brought a systemizing clarity into the stream of Christian thought: Augustine in the fifth century, Thomas Aquinas in the thirteenth, the Reformation in the sixteenth, and probably the twentieth because of the stream of several schools inspired by Karl Barth's 1919 *Der Römerbrief.*

The crisis comes in a shuffling of the pecking order within the church constituency at each new theological drift. The twentieth century opened with Protestant thought tucked rather safely in a body of conservative teachings and Victorian morals, while Roman Catholics also were tightly bolted into the small box prescribed by the councils from Trent to Vatican I. Albert Schweitzer's classic little book of 1908, *The Quest of the Historical Jesus,* was met with such shocked dismay from the church fathers that he became ecclesiastically *persona non grata* and stayed that way for years in spite of his medical heroisms. Even Barth's opening shots went unnoticed for several student generations. Then men in high places began to ask questions that were far bigger than the answers the church and its encircling public were used to. The church was in trouble, and has been getting deeper into it ever since.

The central issue, of course, is the relation of theology to the reality of the secular world. The comfortable isolation of one from the other began to melt as honest theologians saw salvation as more than a pious pulpit platitude, and suspected that it had something to do with the unchurchly agonies of the poor, the deprived, the enemy, and the cocktail party. Because we have for so long held with the ancient Hebrews that the Holy of Holies is no place for vulgar humanity, we all had visceral resistance to the parting of the veil, even though the theologians saw it as a reverse flow, that is, as the holiness coming out to participate in outside life.

So the post-World War II years have been the time of the "shattering of the faith," the development of teachings within the church that didn't jive with "what we were taught." The ultimate and most repulsive offense of theology to date has been the raising of the cry, "God is dead!" No matter what is really meant here; no matter that the cry is raised from within the church by those who are striving to their own discomfort to see the meaning of Christ in an authentic way. It's just going too far. It just proves that the church of today is being ruined by an international, probably godless, Communist conspiracy (say the frightened traditionalists). Or it just goes to show that when you sit down and properly scrutinize the old teachings from an informed point of view, the whole thing is an empty paper bag (say the scoffers).

Now, as always, division occurs within the church. Those who go along with the new inquiries are badgered, harassed, and accused by the conservative majority who in the long run pay the bills that keep the institution solvent. And those who are offended because they don't understand, or because the goals they had in mind for the church aren't being realized, either withdraw or organize brake-locking blocs. This is one of many frustrating factors prevailing when, with the Vietnam paradox paralyz-

58

ing the greatest nation on earth, the church might have a clear prophetic voice. The bases of support of that very church are shaken and fragmented by uncertainty over the nature of its God and the unresolved puzzle of Christ.

If there is a word of comfort from ancient times, it is that in that critical period of some similarity, the church had the same disease. Practically every New Testament writer displays as diverse and unique an opinion of the meaning of Jesus Christ as we can hear today. Indeed, the first five centuries of church history are dominated by what we call the Christological controversies, massive conflicts in the family of the faithful. It could properly be said they knew less about what they believed than most of us today. True, they were willing to suffer for the minority position of their lot and even make heroic witness to their allegiance to Christ, but doctrinal splintering seems to pop out of nearly every page of first-century Scripture and every event in the record of the time.

All they knew, if one were to sum up all the Christian writings of that day both canonical and otherwise, was that a man had lived in their midst who was *different*. By the time of the reign of Domitian, the eyewitnesses were gone and this man was remembered only in tradition that already existed in so many different forms as to be contradictory and confusing. But with this memory was a community that transcended clans and nations, and that community seemed to have a strange power of survival and a core of strong commitment. It was the community and its whole vague body of memory for which they stood, and lived, and died—not its explanations.

The spirit of the church at Thyatira claimed to be the searcher of the inmost heart, and to those who "do not hold these doctrines, for those who have not fathomed the deep mysteries of Satan . . . , I impose upon you no fresh burden; only hold fast what you have, until such time as I come" (Rev. 2:24-25). Theology, even though it is a stringent discipline and a very important part of the life of the church, is only a part of the exploration that the advance guard are making on behalf of all of us. It is not the announcement of eternal truth; it is rather the incomplete information relayed back as to what *some* of the unknown terrain looks like. Remember how badly the Children of Israel were frightened when scouts came back from the Promised Land talking of giants. Yet the new land was their heritage and their destiny, and under the confident but difficult leadership of Joshua the heritage was claimed.

In this day, as in the first century, it is the call of every Christian to be a Joshua, to set about crossing the Jordan into the ominous mystery of the future, with a sense of faithfulness. The click of Roman spears and strident whines of hostile voices were every bit as foreboding to them then as the mushroom cloud and international power blocs are to us. But they lasted it out, and because they did, we have a strong reason to respect theological honesty and keep going too.

The Fifth Crisis: Ecumenism

To the church at Sardis write: "You have the name of being alive, and you are dead. Nothing you have done is perfect." (Rev. 3:1, 2.)

For centuries the word "ecumenical," the literal meaning of which is "of one household," stood for everybody in *our* household. The ecumenical councils that started out to be the unifying and cleansing operations deteriorated into convocations of those who remained loyal to Rome. In the East, the "Ecumenical Patriarch" presided over those who saw things the Eastern way. Even as recently as 1948, when the worldwide Protestant dream produced the first meeting of the World Council of Churches, the meeting was hailed as a great ecumenical event only by a predictable portion of the Protestants, cautiously tolerated by the Orthodox, and boycotted by Rome.

As such, ecumenicity brought no great critical problems. Worldwide confessional families, such as the World Alliance of Presbyterian and Reformed Churches, provided congenial but pleasantly uncompetitive fellowship. But mid-century XX introduced a new turn of events, namely, the unavoidability of the different parts of the church having to recognize each other, overlap, and make way for the whole. Idealistically, it was called a movement of unity, and the trumpets that announced Vatican II sounded as though the whole thing were a brand new idea.

Actually, as Robert Lee points out in *The Social Sources of Church Unity,* interdenominational and interconfessional cordiality was inevitable. The world was producing a kind of society that could no longer tolerate the luxury and the obvious childishness of sectarianism in the old forms. Social problems, such as urban decay and racial injustice, and international quagmires, such as the cold war in the East and the hot war in Southeast Asia, were knocking the heads of the religious hydra together. The merciless exposure of news media, the bland screens of TV, and the freedom of expert commentary were smoking the nonsense out of a segregated and splintered church.

So the ecumenical movement appeared to the church to be the leading of the Spirit. The Holy See replayed the tapes of the Reformation and said, "Well! Of course!" Conversations sprang up everywhere in parishes and schools and social service agencies, and we pointed out to each other how very much alike we have always been anyway, and how sad it is that we never took time to really understand it. Priests are getting cozy and informal about spilling to the public at large how they always did have questions about the mythological "monolithic structure" of their church, and backslapping Protestant ministers are joining them for lunch to say that maybe there's something to having seven sacraments after all.

The crisis is really more acute for the Protestants, for the shape of the whole non-Roman community is engineered around reaction to the Middle Ages. Protestant worship is by and large made up more of elements that were understressed in the Mass than in a full diet of gospel enactment. Protestant government, and especially churchly discipline, is designed more to allow freedoms Rome didn't allow than to delineate a well-balanced and informed community. The result of this is that the winds of change that come from the Vatican are thawing out the pillars of ice that held up the main vaults of the Protestant structure, and what is left is on the verge of collapse.

A principal example is how the Protestant distaste at the lack of Biblical teaching and study in the Roman Catholic Church caused an overemphasis on the "preaching of the Word," making it, indeed, a central sacrament in the life of the church. So now that Rome is reinstituting at the stimulation of the protesters an honest and disciplined regimen of Bible study, the others are exposed as being much more wind and fury than membership involvement or systematic scholarship. Not only that, but Protestantism has very little of anything besides the overemphasis on preaching to offer a newly congenial, inclusive Christian community, for its churches have been more social centers and confirmers of the neighborhood culture than centers of religious discipline.

Over and over, in countless communities across the country, meetings of "Christian unity" are being held numbering many Catholics—clergy, religious, and lay—accompanied by a smaller number of ill-at-ease, red-faced Protestants who are deathly afraid that sometime during the evening some knowledgeable Catholic is going to ask, "Tell me, just what is Methodism all about?" or, "What is the difference between Lutherans and Presbyterians?"

The crisis becomes even more an annoyance when an obviously important social need is upon us and the honest willingness to produce warm bodies and sufficient funds in the name of Christ finds many leading churchmen absent. That big, imposing structure at the corner of First and Main where the town banker went to Sunday school as a kid has such a struggle to meet its budget to run the furnace and pay the office staff that it has no resources to call on for serving the poor or matching strength with strength on an interchurch basis to clean up a bewildered city. The story is getting monotonous: A certain area has four Catholic churches and twenty-seven Protestant congregations. Total constituency comes close to ten thousand communicants. But at that particular moment when the city cries out for a church of compassionate ministry and prophetic leadership, one Catholic priest with fifteen laymen, and two ministers with two dozen helpers arrive backed up with a budget strong enough to provide a half-time secretary. True, the spirit of those who are there is both devoted and commendable, probably even heroic. But the smell of hypocrisy about a church that has proclaimed the universal importance of Christ and sings "Onward, Christian Soldiers" provides a momentary depression. We have so much enjoyed the comfort of a carefully closed-off corner of Christendom that meets our particular tastes in religion that we're not going to let those "ecumaniacs" ruin a good thing.

This is, of course, only partially true. There are occasions when the church manifests a greater unity and speaks with more sincere voice. Like Watts, and Newark, and Detroit, and Chicago, and Memphis, and Atlanta. It was a commendable and gracious gesture for Archbishop Iakovos of the Greek Orthodox Church to sing an Eastern liturgy over the bier of Cardinal Spellman in Saint Patrick's Cathedral, and a few short weeks later to sit in the Ebenezer Baptist Church of Atlanta at the funeral of Martin Luther King, Jr. But it took the universal and all-human drama of death and its mystery to bring it about. In the day-to-day affairs of denominations it was rarer than rare for these old barriers to come down. And, in fact, they went right back up when the burials were over—to await another mystery or tragedy or unmanageable crisis. It is a parable.

The truth is that the church, in all its forms, is unable to decide what to do with the ecumenical mandate. There is a feeling that it is a moral necessity, and here the documents of Vatican II are more straightforward and painfully soul-baring than all the scholarly position papers of the World Council of Churches. But beyond that, any step taken in any direction is so difficult and costly that it calls forth pain and kinetic resistance. For *everyone,* sincerity in ecumenical relations demands more than he knows now.

These words are written by a bureaucrat in the United Presbyterian Church, a denomination in the forefront, vocally at least, of the drive for unity. As a matter of fact, mine is the portfolio of counseling my fellow Presbyterians into ecumenical honesty. The more I work in this field, the more I realize that my communion has a lot to lose. It has developed over the years a strongly knit and somewhat effective political system as well as a large constituency that gives amazingly unified support to an ambitious worldwide program. But ecumenicity means that in sharing these very strengths with other churches, we are going to become less well organized, less effective, and less united. Our theological integrity, expressed in the Confession of 1967, is going to have to be diluted and compromised with brother Christians who see the expression of faith in different ways and consider other emphases to be more important.

So be it. It is becoming increasingly clear that the Presbyterian system is at its best in the context of the Western, Anglo-Saxon, moderately educated middle class. In other settings it is less than adequate. The Latin American temperament finds in Presbyterian polity a wonderful opportunity for division, sectarianism, self-righteous isolationism, and the opening for personality-weighted power struggles. That portion of the Christian tradition that is making the most effective impact on the culture south of the Rio Grande is Pentecostalism, an embarrassment to both Roman Catholicism and historical Protestantism. To be truly ecumenical implies not only a recognition of this fact and an acceptance of this community but a benevolent restraint in the Latin American religious scene. Ever since John Calvin signed the Augsburg Confession of Luther in the sixteenth century, his sons have prided themselves in being truly "catholic and inclusive," but when catholicity means that there will be an invasion of what we have thought of as good taste, we find our sincerity hard put.

The Catholics have their problems too. Liturgical reforms such as the use of the vernacular in the Mass and the loosening up of congregational participation have caused widespread panic. These, after all, were symbols dearly held long before Luther. As one Catholic layman quipped, the only way nowadays that you can tell whether you're in a Roman Catholic church is to ask the priest at the door how his mother-in-law is. And, he comments further, any day that might be changed!

The grand result is a general demoralization and confusion. In the very time when all the other symbols of security have been giving confused signals, the church ought to be the constant assurer, one would think. But lo, in every one of the areas we used to depend on so fully, the hierarchy, or the liberals, or the anti-Christ conspiracy, or whoever, is pulling the rug out from under us.

It's not just the conservative man in the pew who is rocked by ecumenism. Peter Berger, already mentioned as an active liberal churchman, claimed that the ecumenical movement was "simply price-fixing" among similar religious packagers competing for a shrinking market. "Since the Churches increasingly have to take consumer preferences into account in marketing their wares," *The New York Times* quotes him, "in a secularized world this means the Churches are secularizing themselves from within in order to attract consumers."

He comments further that Protestantism is the farthest advanced and has reached a strange state of self-liquidation, whereas the crisis is all the more severe in the Roman Catholic Church. "You can't open the lid on this kind of pressure cooker without the steam shooting up to the roof."

What this line of thought probably represents in the liberal world of cryptic commentaries is a reluctance to see the ecumenical developments in any perspective more hopeful than that which views ecumenism as a natural child of our sociological age. It is a reasoned warning to those enthusiasts who hail the convergence of different traditions as that long-awaited omen in the sky that means the church will triumph after all. The ecumenical movement is not all that big, say Berger and many other historians and sociologists. It's more just a Johnny-come-lately adjustment by a weary church to a competitive world.

From the record, he has a case. From the record, too, the hopers also have a case. Ecumenism was probably the first formal crisis in the church, as recorded in Acts, ch. 15, and Gal., ch. 2. The relationship of the new group to the Jewish community and to the Gentile world was a matter of great concern. There is no doubt that the confusion and hard feelings generated nearly brought about division or even obliteration.

And here we must insert between the lines what the story doesn't tell but retrospect affirms. Above the confusion, and reaching beyond the hurt of divisions, and transcending the childish narrowness, and steering through stumbling strategies was a positive survival factor that was the real characteristic of the church then.

Let him whose mental processes are in working order think on that one a while.

The Sixth Crisis: Church and World
To the church at Philadelphia write: "I have set a door before you that no one is able to shut." (Rev. 3:7, 8.)

Probably the most grievously uncomfortable of all crises in the church today is the uncertainty over relations to the social, political, military, and economic arenas. Purists maintain that the church belongs to a special extra-worldly order that only touches the sphere of secular life at the point of commitment and moral determination of the individual believer. As a corporate body, the church's only function is to set the surroundings for this commitment and carry on those activities of worship and teaching in which a person's subjective relationship to his God may flourish. The social witness, they say, is then adequately carried out through all the other secular and public institutions and private lives of those who are called to follow Christ.

But there are others who, pointing to the welfare program of the primitive church as recorded in Acts, and the collections taken up for the poor in Jerusalem, and the use of political pressure by Paul and his Roman citizenship, say that the church as a whole is called to a type of witness no individual can possibly effect on his own. These heirs of the Social Gospel of Walter Rauschenbusch see the church as a community whose teachings can become valid only when its members are in motion incarnating the love that Christ taught. They feel that Jesus measured his own ministry against visible accomplishments: "The blind see, the lame walk, the lepers are cleansed, the deaf hear, the dead are raised, to the poor the gospel is preached" (Luke 7:22). The church, they say, as guided in the spirit by conscience, is compelled by that very fact to throw itself as a secular force into the balance of the many different causes trying to affect the way of men. They remember that Jesus commented casually one day to his disciples, "And greater works than these will you do" (John 14:12).

At the onset it looks like a polarity unresolvable. The two viewpoints seem to be so contradictory as to create an impasse. It may even be better if this were true, for the picture would be considerably simpler. The church could simply divide into two instead of two hundred groups. The fact of the matter, which becomes evident from a little historical comparison and analysis of the current scene, is that all Christians who have any sense at all of the importance of the church are really on the same pilgrimage going in the same direction. But the difference in speeds of travel and in concepts of the nature of the journey causes the church to be indeed a torn and strung-out caravan in which the different sections have lost communication with or indeed even awareness of each other.

The most available illustration of this situation is the distance between two prominent journals of the day, *The Christian Century* and *Christianity Today.* The former, since pre-World War I days known as a forum for those who believe in "responsible involvement," has been traditionally known as a liberal magazine. This popular label is largely upheld by its editorial policy, which has rather consistently been positive about such things as Biblical criticism, theological dialogue, conciliar and ecumenical concerns, and a gentle satirizing of the older, revivalistic, subjective ideas.

Christianity Today, born since World War II and financed by a cadre of wealthy conservative and loyal churchmen, obviously came right from the womb as a corrective to the "one-sidedness" of *The Christian Century.* Taking as its founding editor a professor from an independent, conservative theological seminary, *Christianity Today* (with a format not strikingly dissimilar to *The Christian Century*'s) has sought out writers and commentators who can give scholarly and responsible documentation to caution, restraint, and subjectivism in social affairs, and play the role of devil's advocate in matters ecumenical.

The strain of a competition that tries on the one hand to give substance to a point of view and on the other hand to give a balanced account in anticipation of the other journal's different weighting, has thrown both papers into unnecessarily extreme corners at times. But even when the two publications are at their most distant and are most sharply conflicting on issues, a little historical perspective shows them to be talking about the same basic subject, in somewhat the same general context, and with the same (though semantically different) goals. Their difference is speed and distance; the trail they cover is the one trail of the church in pilgrimage. A recent editorial in *Christianity Today*, for instance, written by the retiring editor striving to state his stand on civil strife, Vietnam, and the role of the church, sounds very wistfully like an editorial printed in *The Christian Century* just six months before *Christianity Today* was born two decades ago!

J. Howard Pew, one of the founders and subsidizers of *Christianity Today*, has a deep love for and an abiding serious reservation about his denomination, The United Presbyterian Church in the U.S.A., in relation to its worldly entanglements. In an article published in *Christianity Today* (July 3, 1964) and reprinted in *Christian Economics* (February 6, 1968), Mr. Pew maintained that Jesus kept a regal distance from public affairs. "Even a superficial reading of Christ's words reveals that He did not interfere with civil affairs." After quoting the "things that are Caesar's and things that are God's" passage (Matt. 22:21), he goes on: "There's a clear distinction between temporal kingdoms and the kingdom of heaven. The jurisdiction of the state and that of the Church differ. Jesus never concerned himself about Caesar's affairs. Job opportunities, methods of metropolitan government, mass transportation, equitable representation in legislatures are plainly problems for Caesar and not for the Church."

In this persuasive and seriously reflective article, Mr. Pew comes to a conclusion quite consistent with the drift of his own logic: "If the Church as a corporate body should follow through with the economic, social and political programs presented by the United Presbyterian Church General Assembly's Committee of Church and Society, she would find herself in opposition to the teachings of Christ and the apostles; she would ignore the lessons of history; she would despise the finest traditions of the Presbyterian Church and violate the constitution its elders and ministers have vowed to uphold."

Mr. Pew and his followers and his money are not to be taken lightly. They are all powerful, and they are indeed posing the questions that may possibly represent a majority of people across both Protestantism and Roman Catholicism. Nor do I here have any intent or ability to prove him wrong. This is just a rehearsal of the crises of the day, and it becomes even more evident when one sees the situation in which this concerned layman speaks. The issue, for instance, of *Christian Economics* that reprints the quoted article is its own parable of the box all of us Christians are in today. This little paper, also dedicated to the conservative line, includes fourteen articles in the printing of February 6. Other than the one by Mr. Pew, *eleven* of these articles are commentaries on such social, political, and economic subjects as the Logan Act, U Thant, federal aid, wages and jobs, Red China, Yugoslavia, and military strategy in Vietnam! Caesar's concerns, every one!

Even farther to the social and theological right, Dr. Carl McIntire, of Collingswood, New Jersey, heads an adamant resistance movement to every move that the mainstream Protestant Church makes, on the grounds that because of its abandonment of Scriptural truth, the church of today is trapped in its own apostasy. Through his organ, the *Christian Beacon,* he keeps up a consistently critical campaign to discredit such modern developments as the National Council of Churches, the World Council of Churches, religious involvement in civil rights, and war protestations. The curious thing about his expressing these deeply held (and well-financed) convictions is his methodology. He does everything the church he opposes does in item-for-item parallel columns. To oppose the National Council of Churches, he has organized a rival group, the American Council of Christian Churches, whose meetings are held in the same city and on the same dates as the NCC's, with the same items on the docket for the public announcement of opposite conclusions. The picture is unbelievably the same on the World Council of Churches scene; McIntire's group calls itself the International Council of Christian Churches and its meetings . . . You get the point. Where happenings or demonstrations or picketings or marches occur on issues of modern life, McIntire will be there, careful to word his signs as contradictions to the other signs.

Without making any comment whatever on the sincerity of those who wish the church would keep out of the world, it can be said that they're just as deeply involved in it as anyone. And the minute they go into action expressing their beliefs, they are playing exactly the same game as the liberals, using somewhat the same methods, and giving witness to the same underlying moral and religious assumptions.

There is no absolutely right position. Proponents of every side in this quandary have undebatable strong points. The "involvement" crowd is right in its appraisal of Scripture and history, for the corporate intrusion of the church into all the institutions of secular society began with the apostles, even though they didn't know precisely what they were doing, or even want it so. Christian missionaries from Paul to Francis of Assisi to Adoniram Judson to Albert Schweitzer have always given directives to the whole man, involving education, health, and welfare. When churchmen of today look at their own country, indeed their own neighborhoods, and see the same deprivations that compelled David Livingston to go to Africa, they rightly ask, "Why not?" and plead with the church to get to work.

But the conservative's reservations on the side of spiritual sincerity are also well taken. Their cause is upheld from without the Christian camp; Rabbi Arthur Hertzberg (as reported in *The New York Times,* March 10, 1968) in assailing what he called the "nervous scurrying for relevance" feels that social action is detrimental to religion. "That's not the job of religion," he said in a speech at The New School for Social Research. "What people come to religion for is an ultimate meta-physical hunger." Even liberal professor Harvey Cox, author of *The Secular City,* is reported by *Time* magazine in its March 15, 1968, issue as saying in a Harvard lecture: "Once you transform everything into a mission for social action and lose the intrinsic joy of the spirit of worship, you are in danger of losing both. You don't really worship and you don't really serve."

This is no empty charge. There is an underlying sense of deprivation, perhaps even guilt, on the part of sensitive people living in a world of injustice and violence. As one young activist said in Hattiesburg during a time of turmoil, "I'd rather go to hell in motion doing something for my fellowman than to heaven in silent prayer." Saul Alinsky, professional community organizer and social worker, who gladly professes to be a nonbeliever though a respecter of the church as an instrument of social change, explained his own "faith" this way: "If becoming a Christian means that I'll get to heaven, I deliberately count myself out. That means I'll go to hell, where I'll find myself among all the other rejected misfits and poor people of history. So I'll immediately get to the task of community organization to make conditions better, and that will be heaven for me!"

Josef Hromádka is one Christian who has accommodated himself to living in a Communist country. Nearly twenty years ago he wrote: "The Church of Jesus Christ cannot be at home under any political regime nor under any social and economic order. . . . She does not complain and she is not afraid when something unexpected takes place, when horizons are covered with clouds and the earth quakes. She marches quietly and courageously toward the heavenly Jerusalem" (*Theology Today*, January, 1950, pp. 449–450). Years later, he wrote: "She has a particular mission: to go down to the very abyss, where men commit blunders and make inescapable personal decisions. This is exactly where the prophets and apostles have sent her" (*Christian Responsibility*, p. 117).

It is definitely a crisis. For the church even to maintain any kind of integrity as it continues as an institution in the modern world and ministers to it, the interior conflict over that ministry will be severe. And because war convoys must travel at the speed of the slowest ship, unity in the church will demand painful compromise on the part of the sensitive, and a pastoral context in which the more withdrawn can still belong and grow.

All of which makes for the very dream of a new order in which the society will reflect the liberated conscience. This dream and its attendant frustrations were not at all unknown to the apostolic church. Every page of the

Apocalypse rings with it. They stuck it out.

"Let anyone who has an ear listen."

The Seventh Crisis: Provincialism

To the church at Laodicea write: "You are neither cold nor hot—would that you were either cold or hot!" (Rev. 3:14, 15.)

Baptist sociologists call it "folk religion." It is the ordaining of the nearest comfortable cultural framework as being central to religious faith. "We show we are Christians," say the Amish, "by our shunning the ways of this world, the footstool of Satan." This is seen in a folkway of unadorned clothes, horsepower, humble living customs, and a German accent. Members of the (Mormon) Church of Jesus Christ of Latter-day Saints affirm their loyalty to the faith of their fathers by obedience to a "Word of Wisdom" proscribing coffee, stimulants, smoking. It has happened in some degree to every family of the church everywhere, from the Coptic Orthodox Church of Ethiopia hailing its country and emperor as Christ incarnate to the entrenched segregationism of the most primitive Southern Baptist.

In its folksy form, the Christian religion is at best pathetically quaint. The Indians of Chichicastenango in Guatemala use the outward forms of Roman Catholicism to stage their pagan exorcisms, and it is a world tourist attraction. But a West Coast businessman who finds in his subjective Protestant tradition a rationale for protecting the white suburban neighborhood from racial change is playing the same game. And he's just as guileless and simplistic as his Central American counterpart.

It's a case of being neutral to the genuine prophetic religious values and letting the culture speak through the church structures. The place in our modern world where it becomes unbelievably tragic is in the Achilles heel of the era: nationalism. In that the churches have in any way goaded the "My country is closer to God than your country" spirit—and they have, you know—they have been drawn into a demonic partnership. It is the spirit of Wendell Phillips, who said in 1848: "Religion is the most productive, the most efficient, the deepest idea, and the foundation of American thought and institutions."

Czarist Russia required the blessing of Mother Church before every bloody purge; German soldiers in World War I wore belt buckles lettered "Gott mit uns," and the Republic of South Africa explains apartheid in theological terms. The effect is to cast over the household of man the suspicion that wherever Christians gather their higher loyalties to homeland preempt their concern for the whole world. So when church leaders of Communist-dominated countries call for a Christian Peace Conference to be held in Prague, and most of the preliminary papers appear to be unenthusiastic about United States foreign policy, the assumption of most Americans is that "they're all Commies—brainwashed puppets." And when an American church body dares to call the administration to task for moral error in the Vietnam war, the cry goes up (mostly from church members), "Un-American!"

Eugene Carson Blake, General Secretary of the World Council of Churches, at his first meeting of the Central Committee pleaded for what he called a spirit of transcendence. It is incumbent upon a forum of churchmen to transcend their own national and cultural sympathies, their own special traditions, and their personal interests, to lift up the cause of Christ. Blake knew only too well what he was talking about; as an American himself, he frequently found that he was the object of hostility and suspicion by fellow Christians and had seen many meetings deteriorate into accusations and defenses of national stances. When the leaders of world Christianity come together, one would think that the awesome reality of Jesus Christ would overshadow the partisan blinders all of us wear. Nonetheless, the unspoken question always underlying *any* international church gathering is: Ultimately, what matters the very most to him? Is he a brother Christian with a foreign accent or is he really a Russian (African, Japanese, Canadian, etc.) in churchly guise? It is the shadow of this specter that falls across every gathering of religious leaders everywhere.

Indeed, it is this ghostly darkness that falls across all history. One can only wonder with William L. Shirer, in his monumental work, *The Rise and Fall of the Third Reich*, "How did it happen that an ancient and cultural people, steeped in Christianity, pre-eminent in modern technology, who gave us Luther and Kant, Beethoven and Bach, Goethe and Einstein, collapsed into savage barbarism in the twentieth century?" How, indeed?

On the parochial scene, this crisis appears in its most corrosive form as a pseudoreligious nationalism. This is called the "right-wing" kind of church extremism. "America First" as a slogan is bad enough in itself, but the sobering fact is that the phrase is essentially a religious credo. Underneath it lies the "manifest destiny" assumption, that Almighty God couldn't possibly get along without the good old U.S. of A., his chosen servant, whose righteousness he abundantly rewards. Not that this is at all new; all gods were tribal partisans to begin with, even Jehovah. But the deadliness of this nowadays is that those who invoke God to either work his will through protecting national interests or risk losing his most deserving followers tend to pull the attention of vital religion away from those very arenas that need it most.

The spectacular characteristic of the Old Testament is that of a maturing and socially sensitive idea of God that eventually pulls a prophetic minority away from nationalism. Jeremiah, though the most dramatic, is not the first in the succession of men of conscience who invoked the judgment of God upon his faithless Israel, and immediately became the target of shocked indignation for being a traitor. But it is the "traitor" strain that keeps the Hebrew tradition always transcending itself, surviving unbelievable national and moral disasters to be the household into which Christianity is born.

Here one can take passing notice of the strain known to Biblical scholars as the "saving remnant." Israel continues to be an actuality in history not through its major numbers, but by virtue of a small, stubborn, faithful, insistent succession of incorruptible men whose lonely stance has been that of morality above nation, God to be obeyed rather than manipulated, and loyalty to Ultimate Truth at any cost. These have been the only connecting links between the happier ages, and it was with this tradition that Jesus identified himself (Luke 4:16-30).

As the author of Revelation would say, "He who has ears to hear, let him hear." Or, in more modern accent, "Get the picture?"

3

If You *Really* Want to Know the Truth About This World . . .

Having given a rather candid glance at the church and its serious problems, the writer of the Apocalypse turns his eye on the reality of man. A possible subtitle to chapters 5 through 9 would be "This is the way it is—whether we like it or not." It amounts to a sizing up of the ground-zero conditions that the church, or any other force, would be up against if it were trying to affect the way humanity lives with itself. On reading this list of assessments, one is reminded of a modern task force involved in a planning process, surveying the situation to know how to deal with it. An engineering firm considering building a dam across a certain river wants to know *in specific detail* the soil composition, shift pattern, availability of building materials, weather conditions, labor market, and a hundred other factors before it makes a final decision to go through with its plan. Likewise, in the first century, following the first blush of enthusiastic abandon on the part of the early Christians, the whole enterprise had matured to the point that some seemed to ask, "Just what are we up against?"

This is a sublimely perceptive passage of Scripture, especially when the oriental symbolism is replaced by translation into modern idiom. Even though we are not here trying to read into the book an omniscient guide to the twentieth century, it is a major point of this writer that there is a certain emotionally valuable parallel between the first-century Christians' predicament and ours. So, it is valid to capitalize on their understandings of man, many of which are so profoundly true that they are as important to us as to them. "This is the way it is." Even with a dramatically different context (especially a technologically upturned world), in the terms the Apocalypse writer used, it still is the same kind of humanity that responds to the same kinds of honest assurances.

When reading this part of Revelation, one has a sense of being dealt with in respect and truth. The writer is trying to parade in great pictorial strides before our eyes the things we have to face if a new order is important to us. It has the same effect as a visit to the doctor who makes a thorough examination, then sits down and with clarity and courage gives the straight facts about the illness, its seriousness, and what must be done in the light of it. Speaking as he is to a frightened, hurt, weary, bewildered, but still hopeful church, the apocalyptist lays a list of realities right out on the table.

It begins with the famous Four Horsemen of the Apocalypse. These mysterious apparitions gallop quickly across the page with a minimum of textual explanation; their importance to the pageantry is so obvious that no comment is required. They represent the four imponderable basic characteristics of corporate human life. In every case, you can hear the average phlegmatic philosopher cluck his tongue with a resistive "Isn't that too bad!" Revelation simply says, in colorful straightforwardness, "Maybe so, but you'd better take it into account instead of wishing it were different!"

The White Horse (*Rev. 6:1-2*). Strangely, the Biblical

list begins with an amoral, spiritually neutral picture. The urge to conquer, with the willingness to use the sword indiscriminately, describes *all of us*. There is a certain aggressiveness in the human animal that has a thousand different expressions, but most of them come through to the receiving world as the slash of a sword. Nearly every corporate unit of society has its "Alexander the Great" syndrome. The small-city chamber of commerce strives mightily for the success and ever-increasing sales index of the business community. The local high school impresses the town more with its basketball victories than with its library, and the 4-H Clubs spur all kinds of creative learning projects by awarding competitive prizes. Parades, processions, public demonstrations of all kinds, are ways the rider on the white horse releases a certain human dynamism.

This is probably what Freud called the libido. As refined by his disciples, this comes through to us as the thrust of being that is rooted in life itself and that moves into the target areas of context as a means of confirming self-identity and purpose. In that Freud used sexuality as a root structure to supply his whole personality system, it can be carried through even here. Masculinity asserts its authenticity by conquest, femininity by entrapping domesticity, the family by "multiplying and populating the earth." It is a libidinal symbol that makes the artist create a nonverbal communication that speaks with frankness and intimacy something too exposing for words. The housewife is obeying her libido when she decorates her kitchen in fetching colors, and so is the schoolboy who practices his trombone so he can "come on strong."

Konrad Lorenz, of the Max Planck Institut in Germany, maintains that no organism could grow to maturity and reproduce its kind without the pressure of inborn aggressiveness. No oak could pass beyond the sapling stage, no clone of amoebas beyond the earliest divisions, no fledgling eagle beyond the aerie's rim, no human infant beyond its mother's skirts, were we not aggressive. We should otherwise die. Aggression is normal, inborn, necessary.

Taking up the Lorenzian theme, Anthony Storr in a recent book (*Human Aggression;* Atheneum Publishers, 1968) comments: "In adult life, the aggressive drive which in childhood enabled the individual to break free of parental dominion serves to preserve and define identity." It is his affirmation that basic aggressiveness is the positive will to live, and even though in its extreme form it has disastrous aspects, "the drive to conquer difficulties or to gain mastery over the external world underlies the greatest of human achievements."

Men are not sheep. They will find ways to conquer, whether personally, societally, or in the development of awesome national power. The church started off in the naïve assumption that the proclamation of the gospel would be gladly accepted because it so obviously filled the vacuum in the human soul of need for belongingness and moral cleansing. What the disciples didn't know is symbolized in this figure mounted on the white horse: that men had been all too aware of that vacuum for centuries and had been actively setting about to diminish its terror. On the basis of the principle that a good offense is the best defense, we humans have always projected our own insecurities about ourselves onto all kinds of hostility targets, and have brandished the swords of vitality so that we could feel there is indeed a big difference between man and the dumb beasts.

The pronouncement of the good news of God's love doesn't have the clear channel to the heart that the early

Christians expected. Rather, it runs into a whole host of head-on collisions with pieces of the self riding out to assert. This means on the individual plane that the good news finds itself swimming against the current like a spawning salmon in the rapids. And on the corporate level the gospel becomes almost contradictory or even irrelevant, like preaching love to Egyptian soldiers who cannot take their eyes off the Israeli ramparts across the Suez.

The white horse carries an amoral rider, for this aggressive urge in man is willing to use any means to affirm itself. Florence Nightingale was impelled to conquer infections in the Crimea and Jonas Salk to slay the specter of polio by the same strong force that made Hitler's bestiality so compulsive. The moral coloring is a development of the value structure that gives direction to the thrust, but the elementary energy is there whatever way it is pointed.

The lesson for the early church was that it needn't be feared as an enemy of life—just be taken into account. The lesson for our day is that our job is not so much to frustrate or squelch the public libido, but to do what we can to affect it positively. The Ku Klux Klan may capture the loyalty of many who find it a channel to release feelings of self-loathing, status insecurity, hatred. It might gradually develop into a social service organization through education and redemptive association. It is not so much an antihuman organization as it is a very human fellowship afflicted with a moral sickness. One might preserve the body and its strength and yet heal the illness. So are we encouraged to look upon such threats to our middle-class comfort as Communism, Black Power, and the John Birch Society.

We can react to the white steed as we wish. We can quake with fear at the power factor and its evil implications, or we can rejoice at the great enabling strength in the potential good. It's almost a poor man's Rorschach test, with the determinant being our own spiritual health. We read into the symbol what our faith leads us to. Evidently there were enough hard-core healthy Christians who interpreted this reality as for us more than against us.

In our day, when the potential of limitless amoral technology looms up as a Frankenstein's monster, it is becoming easier by the minute to clothe our fears in sophisticated apathy. They didn't then. We don't have to now. That white horse could be on our side, and the rider could be wielding a sword of truth. It's just as feasible as the other way around.

The Red Horse (*Rev. 6:3-4*). No age, no segment of history, no part of the world, is a stranger to war. It is the second of the universal realities. Men will always use power to achieve ends, and nations have ever felt justified to wage war as the ultimate use of that power. It's a serious self-deception to live in this world and ever believe that it is, or can be, free of destruction as the final settler of differences.

The red horse rides across the screen of the Apocalypse because the early church thought that with the coming of the Messianic age war would be no more. It became one of the great disillusionments of the primitive Christians that in spite of their ministry of reconciliation, Rome sent Titus to ravage Jerusalem in A.D. 70. When they felt the edge of the ax on their own skulls and saw their brethren slaughtered in the streets in repetition of the sadness of the centuries, they cried out, "Why?" Hadn't their Jesus said that the Kingdom of God was at hand? The tribulation was sore, the demoralization bewildering.

To them the existence of this word "war" is an answer: War *is*. No matter what healing influences may be brought into the stream of history, no matter how noble man may become, the possibility of war is always several points nearer than our worst imaginings. Anyone who has lived through the 1930's and 1940's realizes how unexpectedly sobering is this reality. I remember hearing a distinguished senator say in 1938 that civilization was too far advanced to go to war to settle what could be settled in conference. He was by no means the only one to be discredited when the incredible debacle of World War II began to unleash its cruel fury in September of 1939.

It's hard to believe, even harder to accept as pertaining to *us*. Most of all, it's hardest for the Christian who insists on looking at the world with a rosy hope and a dream about a humane society. But we of all people, even more than the Christians of the first century, ought to be realists and see the red horse. But just acknowledging it and shrugging the shoulders is not the point. It is, rather, to realize that this is the kind of world, with sickness cleaving deeper into the nature of man than we can ever understand or believe, in which it is our calling to maintain a witness.

So they did, or some of them anyway. And even though the horror of it all is multiplied by the thousands since then, the basic fact is still the same.

The Black Horse (*Rev. 6:5-6*). The marketplace is where a very important piece of the action is. Such is the symbol of the black horse: if you want to have any influence on the way men live, you have to think in terms of economics. Evidently in that day as in all days, true colors came out in the struggle for survival in commerce that weren't quite so visible elsewhere. Perhaps the first-century Christians naïvely thought that somehow the gospel had no relation to the world of products and money, just as so many today think the two worlds should be separate.

But there it is, as the third in the last of "the way things are," for Christians to know. It is a way of saying that you don't know anything about the real nature of the people you're working with until you touch them in the pocketbook, which is a way of meddling with their material security. It provides an unequaled way of shaking everything up so that the real but unsuspected scale of values exposes itself.

Certainly Christians of today have ways of knowing this beyond much doubt. If no other experience has dramatized it, the painful dilemma in the struggle for racial justice in housing reveals almost too much. Here we see people who had apparently always stood for principles of love and fair practices, church leaders and devotees of community harmony, become as hostile as caged animals when their own standing seems to be threatened. The curiously inappropriate conflict of "human rights" against "property rights" has led several cities and states with otherwise liberal traditions to withhold legislation opening housing opportunities to minorities. The 1964 California election is only an illustration of widespread behavior. In the California referendum, the voters by an overwhelming majority amended the state constitution to permit "absolute discretion" discrimination in renting or selling. Even though there had been a remarkable unity among the religious leadership in active and vocal opposition to the measure, in a state where church members are a sizeable majority, the black horse had a far greater influence in the polling booths than the moral principles proclaimed from the pulpit. Eventually the United States Supreme Court struck down the measure on constitutional grounds, providing an ironic commentary on the effect of the church for historians to see.

The writer of the Apocalypse had already seen it and

set it forth as one of the pieces of worldly scenery in which the drama of redemptive Christian love was being enacted. Jesus, of course, had already shown his understanding of the relation between economics and faith by feeding the thousands when they hungered as they listened, by interfering in the Temple courtyard with an economic system that was unjust, and by commenting on the inevitability of poverty. Similarly, missions everywhere have been involved with the economics of justice, from St. Francis and St. Bernard to the Salvation Army and Church World Service.

But even these noble ministries haven't yet caught the full implications of the black horse. It is an understanding of how we are *all* subject to the emotional tyranny of the marketplace that is important. We may make certain decisions and commitments in the atmosphere of worship or human need, but they are always amended by the material setting. In other words, the dollar sign looms large over what we *really* are and over the long-range effective decisions society makes about itself.

A very honest and almost ideal portrayal of this reality was enacted recently at the meeting of the stockholders of a large New York bank, as reported in *The Wall Street Journal*. A representative of a national church agency that held stock in the bank challenged the corporation to reconsider its policies in extending a large line of credit to South Africa. His point was quite clear, that by strengthening the economy of that country the bank was using American dollars to uphold the bastions of apartheid, an immoral and inhumane governmental practice. The answer given to him was classic: "We're in the banking business to make money, not incite social reforms."

Yes, indeed! Prove it can be profitable even in the long run, and we'll talk it over. But if it's just to do a good thing at company expense, forget it! Even the famous Ford $5 day in 1915 and the Rockefeller fringe benefits of 1919 were wise marketplace tactics far more than eleemosynary gifts. True, many industries of today are launching voluntary job-training and neighborhood improvement programs, but they're not calculated to be ways of giving away the profits. Many decisions of policy and acts of Congress rose or fell on signals from Wall Street on economic feasibility, and to quote an unfortunately overpublicized remark, "What's good for General Motors is good for the nation."

The ride of the black horse is not intended to be bad news or to dampen our enthusiasm for the relevance of the gospel to human life. It is rather a piece of extraordinarily valuable information that the church ought to know if it is to survive. Nor should we assess the power of economic reality to be demonic. Like the libido of the white horse, it is amoral—a truth to be used by good or bad. An excellent article recently published in several executive management journals by a printing company insists that American industry has a very important part to play in solving the problems of today's poverty, housing inequities, urban slums, and racial tensions. Even though the underlying argument to the business world for this involvement was its own survival, it was calling for important and desirable goals. The church need not think that the Kingdom has to come *in spite of* the black horse. It can be saddled by wise and perceptive people of moral principle and hard realism.

You don't need to look at the tall buildings of Wall Street and the way they nearly obscure the graceful tower of Trinity Church and then lament that God is crowded out. He can use the frenetic life of the stock-market floor to his glory just as easily as he can use the nearby churchyard, and it's a wise church that knows it.

The Pale Horse (*Rev. 6:7-8*). Of all the harsh realities of this world that frighten the ordinary person, the one Christianity has never surrendered to is death. A symbol of finality, defeat, and utter hopelessness to most cultures, frantically and pathetically covered by pyramids and occult bleatings, it is indeed the common denominator of all mortal men.

It is significant that in the non-Christian traditions the greatest shrines are monuments of appeasement to the mystery of death. The Taj Mahal, the Mayan-Aztec temples, the Alhambra of Spain, Angkor Wat of Cambodia, the Sphinx at Giza and its gigantic neighbors, are all mausoleums. There is something so profoundly imperturbable and inscrutable about this demanding black void that it has become a constant obsession to the living.

It was in the days when Stalin's corpse was still on public view that I was in Moscow and visited the tomb of the Soviet gods. Thousands of us stood in hushed anticipation on the cobblestones of Red Square outside the Kremlin that cool, foggy morning. As we approached four-abreast, the feeling of heavy mourning mixed with awed adoration was everywhere. Inside, bathed in golden light from concealed spots, the bodies of Lenin, forty years dead, and the mustached despot were offered to our vision almost as an affirmation that they weren't really gone. Muffled sobs from genuinely moved Soviet citizens were the only sounds. Afterward, the path led through the little cemetery behind where the heroes of the Bolshevik revolution lie.

Indeed, there is an element of this same heavyhearted wistfulness in many of the burial customs of affluent America. Cemeteries that offer an atmosphere of peaceful sleep are to be found everywhere; morticians prepare their deceased clients to be as lifelike as possible. Most funeral services, including those of the church, omit the references to the finality of death and concentrate on comforting the family with assurances that their "loved one" is alive and elsewhere, a somewhat blasé distortion of Christian teaching.

The church has nothing to fear in the reality of death! The church came into existence because a man died but was not destroyed. It has watched its beloved friends and leaders taken in every conceivable cruel, degrading way, and it felt a new victory each time. It is this world, this lonely frightened world, in which men die alone and defeated, that hides its face from the reality of death. But the Christian doesn't have to. As a matter of fact, in this measure the new technology only increases the Christian's stability. For even though we now can talk about genocide, and megadeaths, and national annihilation, we have only broadened the dimensions of the very same death that the church knows so well.

"If we live, we live to his glory, and if we die, we die in him." (Rom. 14:8.) "Beloved, do not fear those who abuse you, for if they kill the body, what more can they do?" (Luke 12:4.) It mystified the Romans and confounded the Greeks that the church didn't cringe properly in the face of this awesome inevitability. There's no reason it should do so now.

Other Realities (*Rev. 6:9 to 7:17*). Following the four horsemen symbols, the list of undeniable circumstances goes on in a new arrangement of categories. After the major imperatives of life-thrust, war, material need, and death, other considerations are only additional detail, like the color shadings of a master portrait of Creation. In a remarkably human and winsome touch, the writer here turns an appreciative look at the inner relationships and sufferings of the church.

First come the casualties. Traditionally we have called them "martyrs" from the Greek word "witness"; the word was self-explanatory in those days. The picture in the Apocalypse of the fallen saints under the altar was the fact of the time; those who bore a faithful witness were required to pay a heavy price, frequently their very lives.

So it was then. The circumstances now are very different, and the word that describes the sheer truth of this matter is not "witnesses" or "martyrs" but "casualties." The outstanding reality we have right before our faces today is the enormous slippage in the community of those whose commitment carries them all the way through. Not that there aren't heroic instances of people whose lives are offered up as singularly outstanding sacrifices—this is the century of Albert Schweitzer, Albert Lothuli of South Africa, Dietrich Bonhoeffer of Germany, and Martin Luther King, Jr., of America. But at this point in history, when the church numbers in the millions of members, it is more important to be passingly grateful for these and take note of the tens of thousands who spin off from the life of the church in times of crisis.

It was the pastor of a large church in a Southern city, fighting the battle of prejudice and fear, who commented on the passing parade of church members who withdrew their support because of difference over issues: "No army goes into battle without expecting to suffer casualties. What we have going here is a full-blown war. If we were to retreat to a position where we could lose no troops, we would not be fighting the good fight." It is said that over 60 percent of the U.S. population are church members, yet the operative community at work and worship is a small part of that. Even more rapidly diminishing is the number of Christians in mission.

There are in the twentieth-century church several kinds of casualties of a level of importance equal to that of the first-century martyrs. The first of these, for instance, is the category of those who become church members to effect other goals. These only really become casualties when the life of the church is ineffective in challenging them to grow. This may be the majority classification.

A more poignant kind of casualty is the one who with intensive devotion has thrown himself toward the accomplishment of one Christian objective and becomes so frustrated that he becomes embittered or withdraws, feeling alienated or betrayed by the church. Gandhi, perhaps Stalin, may have been this type of lost companion.

There are also those who continue to participate in the institutional structures of the church, perhaps even in leadership, who stultify or disable both the pastoral and prophetic in order to keep the local unit they know best on a limited fraternity basis. These casualties are not only losses in the battle columns but manage to keep the general effectiveness of the attack to a minimum.

Add to these the dysfunctional casualties, good and devoted people who are undertaking the wrong jobs. Many have become clergymen because of guilt or other negative motives, and work out their ministries as sentences at hard labor. Others are decision makers when they know little about the elements of the decisions, teachers when they don't know the gospel, worshipers with no sense of joy. Whereas in the first century the martyrs finally turned out to be an asset of inestimable worth for the courage and faith of other Christians and became sources of legendary inspiration, these casualties may also in the providence of God offer their inert lives and colorless neutrality to be the runway on which a new form of the church takes off. If the new age will require a new form of the church, then those who offer up their lives in the killing off of the old, even by means of mediocrity and the losing of that spark of prophetic hope that is their heritage, are no less heroic even if unintentional.

At this point in the apocalyptic writing, at the opening of the sixth seal, a note of intense sobriety is injected to show that the judgment of God falls on all men, kings and slaves alike. It is an inescapable fact that there runs through history a thread of what appears to be a feeble moral necessity, rising like a giant black whip and laying waste the mighties of empires. Injustice has its mighty backlash, which may prove to be even more unjust and heinous in its own way. But at least of this fact we can be certain: there is a mysterious and unpredictably powerful cycle in the ways of men in which the seats of oppression and depersonalizing manipulation reverse their fields and claim their proponents as chief victims. Such is the world of ancient times. Such is the world of all times. This is the setting in which the church, still stubbornly a community of reconciliation, offers up its own beloved, so often not knowing the dynamics at all, as living sacrifices, casualties.

But it is in this same seal, this same heartbeat of Revelation, that the church proclaims the wonder of its own miracle. Coupled with the only too evident reality of serious and tragic losses, amazingly, *the church is still here.* It continues, survives. The miracle of the church's survival was enough of a glad surprise to the people who heard or read these words in the days of Emperor Trajan; it is a thousandfold more remarkable fact nineteen hundred years later, and thus becomes a main foundation of this book. Stated in impressive symbols, it comes through crystal clear in its meaning in the seventh chapter of Revelation. It was a happy experience to look around and realize that the family of faith had a healthy international root system. Every disease a society can have, had ravaged the church: division, corruption, betrayal, persecution, ostracism. But it was not only alive; it was vigorous and growing!

There really seems to be no logical reason for the persistence of the church through all the imposing ages of the forces of disintegration. Certainly if it hadn't been crushed by powerful enemies from without, it by all odds should have collapsed of its own weight within. A prominent Anglican bishop after an especially quarrelsome meeting of clergy commented, "This is the proof that the church is divine, that it outlives its own leadership!"

Granted, the form in which the church arrived at the modern age may be only a hollow skeleton of what it started out to be. Its imperfections may be so considerable that its ministry of healing an unreconciled humanity is only a feeble gesture. *Yet,* it is! Its pilgrimage through the years, around the world and to every culture, is a matter of undeniable and fully documented record. Its effect on men and nations, good and bad, direct and accidental, cuts the widest swath through the years of any movement ever known. You just can't ignore a fact like that, and from the places of their sufferings in the late first century, they didn't. "These are they which came out of great tribulation." (Rev. 7:14.)

The Pageant Within (*Rev. 8:1* to *13:18*). Christianity deals with all the planes that men live on. When attention has been given to seeing the realities of life, death, history, power, and justice, the most important part of man has yet to be considered. This is the inside, subjective pilgrimage of conclusions and commitments that parade within the living, thinking, feeling, reacting person who struggles to see the world through eyes brightened by a vision of Christ. This is, in fact, the prime subject, for regardless of the way we pose our different fronts and masks, inside we are all involved in a drama of self-dialogue with unlimited dimensions. We continually enact scenes in which we participate with courage and fear, joy and grief, discovery and dismay. This drama, unseen by others, is the basic determinant in the way we decide to perform our lives and the context in which we will insist on reacting to what goes on "out there."

In a time of crisis, the battle is always on the two fronts of the inside and the outside, the near and the far. And though history will record only the outer actions, the reality farthest from the person, it will always be the indescribable, the unreachable, that has been the place, or the event, or the different world of what went on in the inner man that is the first reality. Biographies of great men can only work backward from the observable to sheer speculation about the inner conversations, picking up miserably incomplete fragments from diaries, letters, or remembered intimacies. The vast bulk of this pageantry will remain thoroughly unknown to the rest of us.

Yet, recognizing what men really are, with that incisive awareness that characterizes the early fathers, the writer of Revelation rehearses for us in symbols of high drama what may well be the pageant of his own soul in a time of tribulation, exposing to us the necessarily grandiose dimensions of a Christian's dreams and predicament in a world where most men are afraid of their dreams. Remembering that this was a day when men were far more subject to the gruesome symbols of superstition and ignorance, far less calmed by the assurances of science that molecules and bacteria and chemistry are not malevolent demons, one finds the unfolded seventh seal splendidly healthy. The poetry reader doing his thing in Washington Square, the T. S. Eliot or the Arthur Miller of today, are part of the same fraternity, those who reach into the cavernous jumble of inexpressible impressions and pull out shadings of beauty and inspiration that others can recognize with appreciation far above understanding.

To all men religion comes as a pageant, in glorious clapping of thunder, sounding of trumpets, or perhaps in the rustle of wind through the trees, the creaking of an old house. To some, appreciation of the orderliness and dependability of faith is symbolized in the purring of a well-tuned motor, or the architectural symmetry of a new shopping center, or the innocent laughter of children at play. We live in a variety of worlds, and no matter whether the sound be a song or a noise, some man can hear God there. I have seen men moved to tears by looking at the steel skeleton of a high-rise office building, and others at the roar of a crowd at a football game. It doesn't so much illustrate that we have gods of different importance as that for each of us there is a personal, intimate channel into the place of binding decision, that dark sanctum sanctorum where standards, feelings, and choices intersect. It is the symbols that "get to" a man that move him to come out of his shell and *be*. The wise apostle speaking to his brethren knew this only too well. The whole book of Revelation, in fact, is addressed to the kingdom within, and in this particular passage (Rev. 8:1 to 13:18) is described what might be the contents of several such inner kingdoms.

A man whose whole frame of experience is the twentieth century might undergo the same kind of inner dramatics, be moved to the same intensity, although with vastly different scenery and props to his pageant. Following the "silence in heaven for half an hour," the announcement of the majestic proportions of the universe to him might be the roar of a thousand jet bombers overhead, rattling the countryside with successions of sound-barrier explosions. He may see the umbrella of a mushroom cloud and hear the cries of a bewildered people marching in a thousand-mile line to the gas ovens. He may, as he contemplates the totaled columns of the things he'd rather not remember, hear the snarls of diplomats insulting each other at the conference tables, hear the resentful and bitter defiances of the rioting mobs in the blazing slums of his nearby cities.

The list of woes that unfold before the discerning mind could be for him a procession of unbelievable, haunting, blank-eyed figures, the host of citizens of the Republic of Congo who thought they were recognized at least by the nations of Christian tradition as humans, then felt the sting of bullets in their chests when they rose to claim their place. They could be the eleven million blacks of South Africa and Rhodesia who see their rulers live as kings while they survive animalistic degradation. He could see, with utter disbelief, the resurgence of the same kind of self-protective spirit that brought on the arrogance of Nazism and the debacle of mid-century Germany.

But the whole thing leads into a shaking and monstrously devastating insight when, as he views all these woes of man visiting upon himself the angel of death, he can see himself in the picture! In this pageant, man is not just a spectator; he is a chief figure in the drama. This is what troubled the early Christians to the marrow, that they were men in a world where men, stripped to their fundamental elements, were really animals. The Christians were men, these very men, called to be God by one who was himself man and God. They couldn't see this kind of depiction of the evils of mankind in their own souls without the agonized confession that they too were men. Dr. John Meister tells of his adopted son, whose left hand is mangled and whose face is seared with purple scars, the result of ferocious and cruel fire. And who did it? "I did it," says Dr. Meister, "and you too. He was burned by American troops scourging the Vietnamese jungle with napalm." No one of us, no small group of us, would ever set out to do a thing like that; yet collectively, in the blind and impersonal power we are trying to unleash on our unseen enemies, we perpetrate the kind of events in which it does happen. And we who proclaim the primacy of human values stand just as much to blame for that pitiful burned face as any other human being. This is the kind of realization that a Christian has as he permits the mighty sounds of universal meaning to seep in through the cracks of his own emotional defensiveness.

But if that were to be the whole pageant, the beholder would die or hide from reality for the rest of his life. This again is the characteristic of the faith, that it calls for a real look that persists beyond the sordid point. For up to this point the drama has only set the stage. Only the background of terror and wonder is there; the events of creation's pageantry have yet to unfold. And appear they do, as seen in the twelfth chapter of Revelation, and likewise in the modern understandings.

Since every Christian has wondered about the fragility of the church, whether it could ever really survive a head-on confrontation with the full force of evil man, the battle is enacted here, the adversaries in the form of a woman in childbirth and a red dragon. The conflict is one of harsh and obscene implications, as of course it always is. Modern man is far better equipped from his memory of the recent past to undergo the emotional stress of this part of the pageant. He remembers the way his own Christian forebears used the gospel to justify such demonic things as slavery and colonialism, and how eventually, though subtly, the overtones of that same fragile gospel caught up in the form of conscience and judgment. He knows the effect on the New World of a new gospel that would denigrate Christianity and all religion, and has already seen in the Soviet Union that what appears to be an institutional and political victory hasn't yet captured that part of man which cannot be taken at gunpoint or be bought with rubles. Over and over again he has seen men use power beyond imagination to destroy what has always been felt to be effeminate, only to find it indestructible. So anyone can well sense the emotional tone of this conjectured but so very real conflict. Repeatedly the dragon, though never himself totally destroyed, is unsuccessful in devouring the woman.

Even as the ancient scroll then introduces two more beasts coming up out of the sea to make the terror and the seriousness of the symbolic confrontation more comprehensive, so does today's mind also behold the rising of powerful and fearsome forces whose very appearance makes men tremble. It may well be that for us the first of these beasts is the specter of a technology that may get out of hand. We know with sharp memory that the studies of atomic energy, started in the 1930's as a way of releasing power to heal the wounds of a people laid low by depression, recoiled with horrifying viciousness and slew over two hundred thousand innocent people in two twinklings in August of 1945. We shake our heads in sad understanding as Margaret Mead ponders the "discrepancy between Christian belief in giving and resistance to 'socialized medicine, foreign aid, government approved programs of flood control, etc.'" It has become to us a sign that the most benevolent of intentions can be behind the building of machines that snap to life with unsuspected brutality. We have worked so hard to solve the problems of disease, only to find that each new solution (such as the Salk vaccine) crowds the earth with more survivors to devour the already waning food supply, and throw us into horrible famine. We develop the contraceptive pill to solve the world's problems of birth control and release upon ourselves the dimensions of a new problem in sexual morality that reaches into our own middle-class homes with what Michael Polanyi, using Martin Buber's classic term, calls the development of I-It relationships. We constantly find new ways of tapping the earth's resources of fuel and nurture, only to find that we are using them to power machines of war more than machines of healing.

Indeed, it is a beast whose power is legion, but in our own experience we recognize him. He is the subject of every newspaper's headlines; he is our own reflection in the mirror. But like the Leviathan and Behemoth of The Book of Job in the Old Testament, he is the very worst that can happen to us—he who may even prevail in the next to last battle, but will never be the victor in the end. It must needs be that every one of us entertain him in our secret pageants within, but that in even that intimate rehearsal of the facts of life, we need not be frightened to death. For, as Fosdick says in that superb little book, *A Faith for Tough Times*, "Vitality is mightier than size." The woman giving birth never becomes the dragon's victim.

Nor shall we.

4

Naked Power

Power is always frightening. It *could* be destructive, especially to me. The "progress" of civilization is the story of a monumental build-up of power on many sides. This is a time, as all times are, when power is sought at any cost to survive, to surpass, to reign. The lone individual in our day has the uneasy feeling that no matter where he camps to gather his belongings around him as security symbols, it may turn out to be in the path of some charging locomotive.

The nations lust after power in their own "national interests." So we have military power, a small fraction of which if unleashed would destroy most of us. We have economic power, with gold locked in vaults while millions starve. We have negotiating power, with uneasy compromises that make "peace" really only a guarded standoff. We have political power that enforces tyranny around the globe and keeps the low-caste in their places.

No wonder we are tense! A Negro leader invents the phrase "Black Power" and the whole country is driven on the defensive. So we try to react by organizing our own, hopefully benevolent, power. Poor people are gathering into community organizations as the workingman did into labor unions and the businessmen into guilds before. We have property owners' associations and white citizens' councils, and societies to help the blind, diseased, handicapped, and unprotected. Power as such, then, is morally neutral. It's the instrumentality of getting what we want or need, and anyone who is clever, resourceful, or ambitious can scratch around a bit and find some kind of power.

But that's what makes it so frightening. Anybody can seek power, and there seems to be no underlying guarantee that power will have any special consideration for us as persons with our own little spheres of need and vision. Once it becomes effective, it seems to develop a blindness to those very values that make room for our uniqueness and specialness. Gayraud Wilmore, commenting on a national conference on church and society, writes: "Violence in our land is inherent in value structures and social processes which the Church itself undergirds and participates in as a social institution. The violence which permeates these structures and processes we shall call 'systemic violence.' "

The impersonal blindness of power in violence draws this crisp observation from Wilmore: "Rarely does the Church repudiate such violence. On the contrary, the Church frequently sustains systemic violence with its silence, if not its benediction; with preference for order rather than for justice; with a lack of zeal for the vindication of the victims of injustice."

John of Patmos gives a great deal of space in his work to deliberation on the reality of great power. Parading before us a host of easily recognized symbols of beasts (powers) with horns (authority) and strength (impersonality), he confronts us with the way things are, replete with emotional colorings that little people can't help but have. His terms are the ultimate of his day, dealing with the awesome horror of Rome, the plight of the innocent powerless, the primeval struggles when collective bestiality rises even to the surprise of the most malevolent. Even though the message underneath is one of assurance, that the Lamb is the eventual victor over all the demonic possibilities, the purpose of the writing is not to divert our attention from the terrible conflict but to acquaint us with its unbelievably cataclysmic proportions.

Not that the modern citizen is unaware of these very things in today's world; he probably is a hundred times better informed about the origins and dimensions of the beasts than his ancestors. But the tendency to try to carry on as though it isn't so is ours as it was theirs. And the necessity, in Christian realism, to know our world so that we can see the majestic relevance of a reconciling gospel is probably all the more important to us than it was to them. So, for any honest assessment of the validity of hope for us, a translation of the power passages of the book of Revelation into our day becomes the only way to go.

Eugene Carson Blake recently remarked that the big, brutal clashes around which the greatest amount of depersonalizing power is concentrating in this period are three: the haves vs. the have-nots, the white vs. the nonwhite, and the East vs. the West. Like the three rings that are the trademark of a popular ale, these three arenas are separate issues but overlap just enough to intensify the seriousness for the whole world. None of the six sides, as such, is a "beast," for they represent segments of mankind, each with a valid claim to existence and protection. The beastliness appears in the dimensions to which a conflict makes use of power that devastates the values inherent in a world of peace. It's like an old Hollywood Western movie, where the fight in the saloon between the hero and the sheriff destroys all the furniture, the liquor on the shelves, and the big expensive mirror behind the bar. Evidently the contestants believed their causes so important that consideration of the welfare of others could be counted out; the conflict and its consequences came first.

But of course one needs only to look at the circumstances under which pressure is building up along the frontiers Blake spelled out to see that huge exertions of violence are both possible and even probable. Look, for instance, at Latin America, where three hundred million people will be living in 1975, with a daily average calorie intake of half the normal amount required by health, endemic diseases touching half to two thirds of the population.

In that Hispanic world south of the Rio Grande, more than 50 percent of all people over six years of age are illiterate, with average schooling less than second grade. The annual per capita income is about $290, just one tenth of the U.S. average, and with the inequities between rich and poor figured in, it is possible that three fourths of the total population live on about $80 a year. In addition to all this, the prospects of improvement are quite dim. The sick economies, the unequal distribution of wealth, lack of diversification in agriculture, insufficient capital for internal spending, and a crippling trade system with developed nations comprise a standstill treadmill.

When one stops to consider that fifteen countries of Latin America depend on one major export, with a certainty of decreasing prices on the international market, and that the wealthy families of this region, skittish at the political instability of their countries, take their money to other parts of the world, one can only begin to imagine the hosts of the suffering and the hopeless there. Power in the form of huge and oppressive military machines, costing two billion and more dollars per year, used by the ruling elites to preserve the intolerable *status quo*, can only make matters worse. And finally, the galloping inflation in this part of the world confirms the suspicion that the poor are more numerous and destitute than they were twenty-five years ago.

Now, then. What is power? We may find out the hard way before we fully digest the signs of the times. Power exerts itself in different ways. It brings pressure upon a society or a country or a person to change his ways; it forces conformity or obeisance by means of everything from subtle suggestion to outright violence. What defines it as power is the fact that it is able and ready to trot out whatever will win the day to effect the result. Over and over again, modern man is taken by surprise at the necessity on the one hand and the willingness on the other to come to violence—sheer, raw, cruel, devastating, life-destroying violence.

The series of expensive and devastating riots that have been sweeping American cities because of the demonstrative resentment of the Negro underprivileged has come as a shock to most Americans, and for that matter, most of the world. Somehow we thought of ourselves as among the most enlightened anywhere, and believed that our forms of government and voluntary do-gooders were doing enough to convince those poor folk that someday anyone who deserved to have what we have could get it if he went about it in the right way. The report of a Presidential commission to investigate the cause of unrest, which clearly proved that the violence did indeed come from the people of the slums and that it was nobody else's idea or the result of instigation from some outside conspiratorial force, proved nearly incredible even to the President himself.

All of which can only stimulate a deep wonderment and some poignant sadness that the insensitivity of a culture can be so rigid, that thousands in our midst, co-workers and neighbors or at least sharers of the public domain, are undergoing such deprivation and degrading heartbreak that the only way our attention can be commanded is by open hostility. One has the picture of a man watching another man with his head under water, not thinking much about the fact that his foot is on the back of the submerged neck, and wondering faintly why he doesn't get up. The one in the water will certainly drown if he is not let up. First he waves his arm behind his back above the surface. Then he wriggles his body to try to free himself from the oppressive foot. If no relief comes, there is only one thing to do as a matter of final desperation. He finds a rock on the bottom, and reaching around with his free hand, he drives it into the face of the man on top. The incredible touch is that the first offender sits back on the beach with a pushed-in face and a reaction of surprise. "I didn't know he felt that way about it. Why didn't he tell me instead of hitting me?"

Stupid ass! Couldn't you see he was in no position to talk? No, the fact is you were so preoccupied with your own matters you never realized the implications of your casually placed foot. But now you have felt the result of the power of self-survival, and from now on your relationships with others will never be quite the same. This is a world of power, brother, and it can get quite nasty if it has to.

It takes no great wisdom to look at our world and predict that the lid is going to blow in several different directions soon. Power will amass where it is needed to right massive wrongs. There are a thousand igniting factors to this tinderbox, but for purposes of illustration just consider the one of the transistor radio, bringing to every far-flung village a picture of men rising up to claim their rights, their portion of a mysterious world of affluence somewhere. See the listeners reason that any action at all, no matter how brutal, would be an improvement over the dire circumstances of malnutrition and suffering; then stand back to see what one clever despot could do with it. No wonder there have been over forty major revolutions in our own hemisphere this century! And if the overlap of Blake's three categories becomes an interlock, as it probably will, we will see more beasts arise than any technicolored dream could possibly produce.

There is a strong temptation to stand to one side in any situation of misused power or chaos and with a cluck of the tongue and a sad shake of the head feel apart from it. It is an interesting fact of record that at the Nuremberg trials not a single Nazi official ever confessed that he was personally responsible. "It was their fault." Or, "I only followed my Führer, as was my duty. To do otherwise would be treason." Any system of power is impersonal, big, ambiguous, and no matter how cruel, isn't "my fault." It amounts to one of the very deepest problems of moral philosophy, whether there ever can be corporate sin made up of a sum total of individual innocence.

The ancient wise Christian writer who called himself John felt that the early church ought to be aware of this problem of corporate guilt. One of the beasts in Revelation is clearly the state, Rome. Not intentionally demonic, for everyone knew that it had spread a system of citizen protection and a sincere regime of justice that was more benevolent than most of the colonies had ever known. It wasn't an empire that exploited its subjects as despotically as the earlier conquerors had done. Indeed, the new channels of trade and international commerce had brought a fairly comfortable prosperity to lands formerly destitute. The Roman eagle, though slashing with sharp talons when unduly disturbed, was not seen as a vulture so much as a watchbird. The early church knew this but also knew that in its vast coverage of a devious and multicultured empire, its sheer impersonality could be bestial, insensitive, irrational, and unpredictable.

So the beast rose from the land in terrifying majesty, commanding the fealty of all its subjects in a jealous command that, even though intended to stabilize the security of the state, invaded the Christian conscience in a painful way. Obedience to the state was one thing the Christians could tolerate, but adoration of it as divine, going through the motions of public adoration, was quite another. The beast is nationalism, and it strides the earth today a thousandfold more terrifying than then, supporting its might by wresting from its people more than a regime of any kind has the right to ask. Its demand reaches deeper into the soul than we think, at times pitting us—even those of us who try the hardest to resist it—against humanity itself.

Karl Barth, who resisted the idolatry of Nazism to the point of exile from his native Germany, came to a more accommodating position in relation to those Christians who must live under Communism. It is a temporary order, he maintained, and the Christian by his submission to or participation in such a country bears witness to this temporary character. But the state is constantly tempted to claim more than a temporary commitment. Every state, although what it *is* in the sight of God is defined in Rom., ch. 13, in fact moves between being a valid authority and being the beast from the abyss in Rev., ch. 13. There can be in history no totally demonic state; always some remnant of providential order clings to the worst tyranny. But neither can there be in history an ideal state, as in Rom., ch. 13! Barth cannot tolerate total submission to any state and maintains that resistance to injustice is a form of intercessory prayer.

That damned beast gets so deep under the skin! I sat at dinner one night at the table of Alexander Zenovitch in Leo Tolstoy Street, Leningrad. I hope this use of his real name brings him no harm, because I want to stress that he did nothing at all disloyal to the Communist ideology of his country. Nor did I, in anything I said or did that night, betray my beloved United States. That, of course, was the sickness of the evening. We were each so victimized by the strong emotional riptides of the cold war that it was impossible to relate as humans sharing the predicament of man. He, his wife, and charming teen-age daughter were earnest, disarmingly friendly, and thoroughly candid. Though they disclaimed any connection or interest in the Christian church, their value structure and even vocabulary were deeply affected by the Christian influence. He was most curious about and somewhat troubled by the "warmongering" attitude of my country and certainly had a valid talking point in the placement of American bomber bases circling the Soviet Union. I was uneasy about the open threats of the Soviet hierarchy and Communist dogma, which made no bones about hostility against the U.S.A. The evident fondness we found for each other as persons had to remain obscured by our two-way defensiveness, in which we were mutually at fault. It was only afterward, in retrospect, that I realized my own conditioned reflexes were more obedient to world politics than to what I had always thought to be a liberal universalism transcending all other loyalties. This beast, this Roman beast, this chauvinism, was for me in a time of aloneness in a foreign place a greater power to invoke than a nondefensive love of persons. That's why Revelation correctly calls nationalism a beast, and that's why its power is so impersonal, so brutal. If it can cause this kind of antihuman alienation in single units, what can it do when groups and masses become blind "national interests"?

Afterward, I read in a book by Charles West (*Communism and the Theologians,* p. 378; The Westminster Press, 1958) a wonderful analysis of this very same problem, and was especially touched by this passage:

" 'Why do you go to church?' a Communist functionary asked a country elder.

" 'Three reasons,' replied the elder. 'In church I am treated as a human being. In church I don't need to be afraid. And in church I hear a free word spoken, and it makes me free.' "

Everyone should have the opportunity of a day in the gallery at the United Nations, especially during the meeting of the Security Council working over a new crisis. There they are, the distinguished and loyal servants of the world powers, outstanding individuals in their own rights, having to be the messengers of mysterious invisible dragons called "my government." When they speak, the flash of man-killing lightning and the peal of depersonalizing thunder rattles the room. No, not in the oratory, which is usually dry and pedantic, or in the demeanor, which looks more like a chamber of commerce banquet. But it's there, brother, it's there. And it's a good thing it's there too; far better the flow of powerful words than the same conflict unleashed in the sky over the cities!

This is the point of its mention in Holy Scripture, and

writ large inside the heart of the Christian in this world. Power is a fact, immense power that impels millions of lives toward good or bad. National power is the order of the day, as it was in the days of Rome, and the horns of authority, the ability to carry out the power into life, and fortune, and conscience, and moral conviction, is something everybody has to live with. Whereas it is expected that most people will accept national power unquestioningly, letting its injustices happen because that's the way it is, the Christian has become so sensitized to a sympathy for all men that he is always hurt when this power crushes anyone.

Well, what about it? Should the church ever try to inject itself into the power scene? At the United States Conference on Church and Society in 1967 at Detroit, an extension of a National Council of Churches study, one discussion group reported: "We proposed that the Church needs a theology of power adequate to the time in which we live. We urged that the most outstanding theologians and lay members examine the disjuncture between the Church's actual use of power and its traditional disavowal of power. It was also suggested that the Church needs to bring critical theological reflections to bear on the nature and use of power in corporate and personal structures in all areas of life."

In that the church of Jesus Christ motivates men to action that reflects faith, it already is in the business of power. Gayraud Wilmore comments: "The Church needs a theology of revolution which takes seriously the meaning of what God has done and is doing in Jesus Christ." He maintains that whatever we do from this should emerge primarily from theological considerations, that is, from our faith.

It is a situation nearly unendurable. We have to live in

a world of untold suffering and distortion of humanity, and because of our convictions we just can't keep aloof. It doesn't seem fair for us to be cast into a world of such oppressive and unrelenting unconcern for the things that matter so much! We don't have the alternative of turning our backs and saying the whole system is evil; we are part of the system. Nor do we have the luxury of turning off our sensitivity; our Lord bore this very burden of care clear to the cross.

This was their problem then, too. Somehow, in ways more mysterious than analysts can figure out, the Roman beast had its day and fell into oblivion, while the church, powerful in ways unexpected, grew and lives on. So the word of direction that comes to us from the gospel, articulated in Revelation, this dramatic writing of old, is for us to stay with it, stay vulnerable, stay caring, stay loving, and never, never, turn our back on the reality of what's going on. For to us in this situation is given no magic relief that lifts from us the responsibility to be persons, no diverting dream of an anesthetic, otherworld dream. To us, rather, is given the gift of hope. Mightier than naked power, mightier than Caesar, Christ the Lamb of God is King. Even more, says this writing, he is in history with us. His presence can give us that added inducement to believe in this world. It is his world.

5

It's Our High Calling to Stick It Out

It may sound rather odd, but I have to say that the book of Revelation is a very earthy book. This-worldly.

To be sure, the church of the ages hasn't always taken it that way; its word has been much the opposite: other-worldly. There's no way to be sure about how the first-century church took it. Very likely many church members saw it as talking of another order. However, as I read into its symbolism not only the apocalyptic mind-set of that day but the years of history they couldn't see, it comes through to me that instead of relieving the suffering church from any responsibility for the world, it really pushes us all right back into it.

When, in the drama, that climactic moment arrives for the Christ to appear, he is standing *on Mt. Zion,* which is closer to this earth than where he was last seen at the ascension. The gospel he brings by the flying angel is for the inhabitants of the earth, and the description of a remnant community who were singing a "new song" and were sealed "on earth" is a here-and-now kind of picture.

In all honesty, it should be said that one can read into this either this-worldly or that-worldly imagery. Again I argue that the context of the first century and the context now, after eras of splendor and agony, lead some of us to feel that here, in this world, is where we belong, here is where the church fulfills its destiny, here is where the singular beauty of holiness pierces through the pain most meaningfully.

The momentum of the strongly moving pageant points us this way too. From the feeble immaturity of the newly born church, through the powers and forces of this world, with a stopover to glance inside the trembling individual trying to find the sources of courage, the subject suddenly becomes the church on earth, and behold, it too has power! The gospel has a might of judgment that pertains to all the ills of men and imposes on all mankind a strong new force of condemnation and reconciliation.

John Wesley, it is said, was once asked what he would do if he knew he had but one day to live. He answered that it would be a day much like all the others, except that he would work a bit harder, try to see more people, confess the Word to larger numbers, visit a few more sick, and then go to bed a half hour early. One can say that that was the mood of an irrepressibly optimistic man, as Wesley was during his last fifty years. But optimism, or faith, or stubbornness, or whatever it may be called, is what you make it. He could have a certain amount of emotional security in living that way and feeling like that, because he felt that that was what he was here for.

Such is the real majesty of the Mt. Zion passage. Instead of a host of assurances that life isn't really all that bad or that we'll all get a rich reward in heaven for sticking it out here, this scene tells us we belong here. Its assurance is that we've got more going for us than we think. There is a quality of blessing that God visits upon his worldly family that may not relieve the sting of hurt but may make us feel better about belonging here. Death?

"Blessed are the dead who die in the Lord." (Rev. 14:13.) Hostile nations? "Fallen, fallen is Babylon the great!" (Rev. 14:8.) Powerless? "The kings of the earth . . . will weep and wail over her." (Rev. 18:9.)

The early church may be like the eldest child who has gone out into the world to wend his way, found it lonelier and harder than he thought, and come home for sympathy. But his father meets him at the door like the angel with the flaming sword at Eden, saying, "You belong out there now." It turns out to be an emotionally and spiritually important event—to be firmly and lovingly rejected at home, that is—for it reinforces the realization of where the arena of his life really is. I firmly believe that the Apocalypse is written to reaffirm to the church where it really belongs, to counteract the escapist dreams and reality-denying myths of an otherworldly heaven. The story rather bears this out, for a new determination to survive seems to set in about the beginning of the second century, enduring to the edict of toleration by Constantine in 313.

The whole force of the Jewishness of Christianity points toward an insuppressible admiration for creation, an adoring respect for this world. When Jesus chose to identify himself with the prophetic tradition of his people in his own home synagogue, he put the whole meaning of incarnation where men live, hurt, disobey, repent, succeed, and fail, instead of where fantasy dreams and fear seek escape. During those periods of history when the church was feeling especially sorry for itself and withdrew with a closed concept of society, it was like a time of suspended animation. True, it may have been a preserving tactic and therefore good in its way, but hibernation is only half living, if that. There are times when no matter how precarious it may be to be very much alive, it is more important to live now than to "run away and fight again some other day."

Now let us try an experiment in historical patience. First, relax for a few hours with a fairly easy book on geology, noting with what immense periods of time the crust of our earth arranged itself for our occupation. Then, after a few days to let the fascinating adventure of mesozoic activity seep in, take out a book on anthropology, watching the eons and millennia roll by as life proceeds from the mud to the marketplace. By this time, with time out for hot baths and long unhurried walks, we will get a very small sense that big developments happen slowly. Next, a survey of recorded history, from the Mesopotamian valley, down the Nile, up the Yangtze, along the Ganges and the Mekong, around to the Rhine, the Thames, and the Mississippi. Acceleration is now setting in, almost in machine-gun style. But even so, man still has his roots in a long and deliberate process, and not everything taking place nowadays is the result of that any more than it is the process itself, still going its patient way.

With this preparation, now turn to religious history and note with some interest that the time from the pre-Abrahamian roots of Judaism to Christ is just about as long as the time from Christ to the present. No, there's no superstitious or numerological conclusion in mind here, just a line of thought that could make us look ahead somewhat less hurriedly. Here's the way it seems to me: the whole experience of the Christian church so far is only a prelude to its coming of age. I cannot help feeling that the development of international and technological pressures has called the religious community to its most important relevance. Corollary to that is the feeling that the two thousand years of Christian life have been mostly preparatory for this and future times. Perhaps it could be called only the overture; the curtain is only now beginning to rise on the real drama of the church in the world.

Look at the church! Indigenous now to every nation on earth, though a minority everywhere, it is just beginning to discover its self-consciousness as relevant to the world. Like an adolescent boy who glances in a mirror to see the developing man, the church has peered into the events of today and seen a place for itself that had been overlooked before. Divided into pitifully childish and competitive fragments, the church senses a new unity emerging everywhere. Formerly naïve and frightened of the noise of the common tongue, alien to the streets and a willing tool of nationalism, now the church has a new small feeling of confidence in the power of the gospel to nations and societies. Once captive to ethnic and cultural expressions, now the church has grown a sophisticated universalism that sees across color lines and habit lines and language lines with understanding and compassion.

There is just as much evidence, if not more, to feel that the church is just getting started and equipped in its ministry to this world as to think it obsolete. When Peter Berger predicts that "by the 21st Century, religious believers are likely to be found only in small sects, huddled together to resist a worldwide secular culture," he may be right in a sense. He's too valuable as scholar and prophet to be taken lightly. But mayhap that is the form that the centuries produce, and it may well be the form that God uses to reach the world he loves!

This is the important core of the call. God keeps putting the church back on the front lines where it belongs, whether it really wants to or not. The way it arranges itself to do his job may not be necessarily the traditional way of the past. To put it in the terms of the modern planning technician's jargon: Proper procedure calls for thinking from *purpose* to *objectives* to *goals*.

The *purpose* is the whole reason for being in business. The church's purpose is to be a community that basks in and reflects the forgiving love of God, so that all its contacts have the quality of reconciliation. Through the years it has become evident that in different places and different times, the little community works to that purpose in very different ways.

Reasonable strategy says that from the purpose derive certain *objectives,* and these are changeable, flexible, according to the local conditions under which we struggle to achieve the purpose. Leslie Weatherhead used this approach in his magnificent little monograph, *The Will of God.* It was God's purpose, said Weatherhead, to save man. Local conditions made it necessary for the objective to be the cross, but it might as well have been any of several other ways and it still would have contributed to the purpose. Weatherhead continues his pastoral word by saying that it is still and always God's purpose to be redemptive and that to permit a world of suffering is a part of the necessary means, not a defeated and futile end in itself.

So the church has its purpose and among its temporary objectives are organization, theology, ministry, and sacraments, all of them dispensable if more up-to-date objectives can serve the purpose better. From objectives one develops *goals,* which fall into the "What do I do now?" category. In metropolitan Kansas City, the different denominations have formed a council for teamed ministry to poverty areas. This is a program goal. The founding of a lay academy in Holland is a program goal—expendable, flexible. Even the building of a huge cathedral-type structure at Fifth and Main in Cornville is only a program goal, hopefully a way to fulfill purpose, but only hopefully, not certainly.

Only with this kind of perspective can the church adjust to the ages; and this is what seems to be called for by the book of Revelation. Strangely, occasionally miraculously, the church has made those last-minute improvements in its program goals that saved it from complete idolatry to the goals themselves. The early Reformers felt that nothing short of complete repudiation and discrediting of the Roman Catholic Church would give glory to Christ. Consequently, a deep anti-Catholic bias has been one of the characteristics of Protestantism, and "back to Rome" was the equivalent of total surrender to Satan. The issues and undercurrents of the Presidential campaigns of 1928 and 1960 show how deep the feelings yet run. But in a world where international and domestic crises are throwing a cruelly bright light upon the irrelevance of such a rift, both Rome and Geneva are honestly counteracting the infections. This can be done because purpose is more important than objective, and program practices always are only passingly instrumental.

An elderly Jewish woman tells of a commitment made early in her life always to have Christian friends at the family table during Passover. This is, she warmly confides, a continuing memorial to an order of nuns who saved her life in an eastern Poland village during a pogrom. The sisters hurriedly collected all the Jewish children of the town into their little chapel as the rioting mob swept through the streets. Barring the door, making the children lie on the floor, under the seats and the altar, these holy women told the marauders an outright lie about a worship service that must not be disturbed. The violence went elsewhere; the children were saved and secretly transported to a convent for care until the turmoil subsided. This is a case where purpose was achieved while program goals (sanctity of the altar, truth-telling) were quickly revised. The fact that it can happen and occasionally does is an assurance that the Apocalypse is accurate in its description of a living, reconciling, enduring community of faith.

The congregation of the Second Methodist Church in Vienna had just completed its postwar reconstruction in the fall of 1956. In the place of the old inadequate building, these good folk had through great determination and sacrifice built a lovely little chapel only a few minutes' walk from the Opernring. It was tasteful, inspiring, and an architecturally proper witness to the existence of a contemporary Christianity. Then the abortive revolt in Hungary exploded and within hours the streets of Vienna were teeming with homeless refugees of all ages and family groupings. The pastor and helpers immediately threw open the doors of the new sanctuary and by nightfall the place of worship was a dormitory housing travel-weary, anxious, emotionally overwrought people taking up nearly every square foot of floor space. When Sunday morning came, astonished members of the congregation arrived to find there was no room for worship. This resulted in a lively dialogue concerning the purposes of the church, with strenuous representation of all sides, culminating in the continuance of support for refugees and the building of an annex to serve as a permanent dormitory.

But these illustrations are too obvious and too simple. What they show is just the near edge of the sea of profound problems of regrouping to do the job today. The century's outstanding example of this so far is the tenor of Vatican II, which acknowledges blame on the part of Rome for some of the tragic alienation among Christians. With the symbol of Vatican II, many kinds of difficult slippages in the ice pack are made possible.

Every age has its peculiar goal needs for the church. In the same way that the Middle Ages needed a rigid structure of dogma and discipline, imbedding Christian values deep into every arena of life, the modern times call for an elasticity and mobility for the Christian community, in which yesterday's stability can become rightly obsolete today without prejudice.

Ecumenicity as a concept can remain a fresh and renewing development of the church only as long as it represents constant, perhaps even daily, change. As a responsible sense of unity creeps over the church, every denomination realizes that surrender and compromise are among the first steps. Buildings, budgets, personnel, even the family vocabulary, will be subject to inconveniencing reuse. A way of glimpsing the demanding significance of this is to imagine a Catholic priest surveying his five-year-old basilica with its canopied central altar, saying to the other members of his team ministry, "And this will be a gymnasium . . ." Or an itinerant evangelist from Oklahoma cheerfully surrendering his tent and benches to shelter striking migrant workers in California. Picture the General Assembly of the United Presbyterian Church voting to turn over $100,000,000 of endowments to a United Foundation under the administration of the Cardinal Archbishop of Chicago!

Within the last decade a new mobility has come upon the church that makes just about anything possible. Just as the advancing Communist host in China drove whole institutions to pick up and move a thousand miles to adjust to the new day, so have the circumstances of modern life caused the church to rearrange itself. Somehow one feels the air crackling with the possibility that it's actually going to happen.

We have to be careful to see every development as a contributive stage rather than as a completed goal. The Consultation on Church Union, now involving several midstream Protestant denominations, is of monumental significance in the *interchurch* area but only a minor part of the *ecumenical* scene. The Consultation is a new step in church history because it begins the process of merging communities of different governments and theologies. But in the totality of the world need, this effort is only a microcosmic part of the effective relationship of gospel and world.

The new and powerful part of ecumenicity in this century is the witness to the secularity of the gospel, and the other side of the same coin, the sacredness of the profane. Whereas the church has held a self-image of being the only community of trustworthy reflection of God's will, we now see that any agency can be the divine channel of justice and love. The uniqueness of the church is not to be found in its franchised dealership of truth, but in its sacramental celebration of the joyful mystery of forgiveness and redemption. Therefore, *ministry,* formerly restricted to the work of the church in the world, now also means the way the world responds in kind to itself.

Ecumenicity, then, means the releasing of the church from its own institutional tunnel vision so that it can relate freely and redemptively with all mankind. If this means coalition with nonreligious agencies to effect a better society, then let it be so. Let the Roman Catholic Diocese of Rochester donate $100,000 to a community organization program for poor people. Let the National Council of Churches promote a Delta Ministry in the impoverished South, and when the funds from governmental sources are politically strangled, let the church carry the plea for involvement to the whole concerned world. Let there be open conversations and shared personnel with Black Power groups, committees to advocate humane immigration legislation and labor unions. Let there be a direct connection between the prayer of dedication at the presentation of offerings on Sunday morning and the bringing about of an ordered society.

This is what might be coming through in the image of the Lamb whose feet are solidly on Mt. Zion, on this earth where man lives. The pictorial language is not at all vague. It tells of a tremendous influence that the community worshiping this Lamb is called to wreak. It is an influence of judgment and reformation and reconciliation, bleeding all the while. The emotional flavor of the Apocalypse is that of a sufficient assurance to the church that even in its suffering its relation to both the Kingdom of Heaven and the world is still on.

What may be the most massive moral problem for Christians since World War II is challenging the church as these words are written. A struggling, nascent nation is dying in the womb in Africa by mass starvation. Six million people are besieged and several thousand innocents die daily because of the immoral intransigence of brutal civil war. Because of the diplomatic impasse, intervention on humane grounds by other nations is impossible. But the religious community, led both by the resources of the official establishments from Rome and Geneva and by the voluntary sharing of millions of caring believers, knows no such barriers. The churches of Scandinavia and Holland have provided a fleet of planes and equipment, and from all over the world food and medicines are being sent. Since the blockade is total, high risks must be taken just to bring food to hungry children, but the moral necessity is unavoidable. Before the tale is completely told, the number of planes shot down and lives lost will be grievously high, but the day demands no less.

It is this placing of the body—the warm, incarnate,

physical apparatus of the church—in the dangerous chasms that is the mandate from her Lord. The honest truth of the matter is that as yet there is only a mere suggestion of such risk-taking in the common life of the church that is called to be the Lamb. Small as it is, the authenticity of that very little bit validates the whole doctrine. With this start, this small scattering of samples, this noble array of possible models from the past for an extraordinary future, an unlimited host of possibilities unfolds itself before the mind's eye.

The field of economics alone is revealing. The institutional church has dug into the local scene with vast resources. In Klopfield Corners, there are seven Protestant churches and two Roman Catholic. These societies have a total money flow per year of about $350,000 for local programs and $180,000 for others, and a basic capital worth of over $1,000,000. There are twelve trained full-time professional and six clerical workers on the combined staffs. Most represent denominations with endowment backup into the millions. This is remarkably advanced from the first-century existence as a community of poverty. Of course, a paralyzing network of cobwebs has to be dealt with to even dream of releasing some of this wealth for mission, but there is not anywhere another movement related to evangelistic and humanitarian concerns that has this kind of resource.

What may hopefully come to be an avalanche has already started. A large church in Pennsylvania mortgaged its property for two thirds of its worth and gave the money for community organization among the poor with no strings attached. National agencies of several denominations are investing their endowments in the economies of so-called underdeveloped nations at high risk and low return. Even though these funds, impressive in themselves, are comparatively tiny in the world economy, they represent an outsize influence on world opinion. In today's values, one's money on the line is the equivalent of bodies.

The so-called Christian education of the churches is another economic amazement. A survey of Protestant facilities in the Seattle area showed a use factor of rooms available for teaching the faith to be .0068 percent of the total possible use. In an age where training for jobs, for organization of community leadership, for centers of social service, are of nearly revolutionary importance, this represents a potential for mission of vast proportions. And even if the church in Klopfield Corners wanted to reserve its physical properties for traditional teaching use, the possibility for local lay academies to indoctrinate for evangelism across denominational lines, considering the faculty already in residence, is several hundred times above present use. An impossible dream? Unrealistic in light of present traditional intransigence and parochial inertia? Very well. Downgrade all this conjecture by 80 percent to be realistic and conservative, and there will still be the resources for revolution. Only 7 percent of the colonial population participated in the 1776 flap; only 3 percent of the Russians in the 1917 to-do. Sixty percent of the U.S. population are supposedly church members, and to take the four-fifths discount I suggest yet leaves a healthy 12 percent of the country!

But can old patterns be broken in time to get into the action where it is needed? I believe so. There is a steadily intensifying desire inside the church to get on with the job. And there *are* new patterns emerging, you know. At the Detroit conference discussed earlier, another report told that one discussion group committed itself to a strategy of "voluntary, disciplined groups as a crucial means for developing power for change in the Church and its witness in society." A commentary on this report notes: "This was an interesting development because the group had, after much agony, decided that each of us has some power and that the combination of small groups of people could be a leavening force. It was suggested that such groups center their interest on specific issues in society and the Church and seriously commit themselves to both the Church and a segment of society beyond the Church."

Some call it *ad hoc* churchianity, others a form of churchly guerrilla warfare. My term is the updating of the medieval holy orders. Whatever its name, it opens a whole new way for the loyal churchman to express his faith and shake off the strangulation of tradition. Contemplate the possibility of *disciplined communities within the church addressed to specific functions.*

First, a little bit of oversimplified history. All of us are aware that the ascetic movement in the early church was the direct result of the insoluble dilemma of trying to live as an eschatological Christian in the world of time and space. In the limited lore of that time, there was confusion about how the church and the world could resolve their different spheres; the tension became nearly intolerable. A small number of Christians felt that escape from the world was the only answer, and to these solitary, cave-dwelling, prayer-muttering, flagpole-sitting recluses the church imputed a certain amount of worth. The second stage of asceticism, which came along when the church had about three or four more centuries of wisdom under its belt, had some different characteristics. True, there was the same problem, namely, the accommodation of the church, with its eternal message, to a very temporal world. But there was also the mature determination to find ways to be loyal to Christ, bless the world in

His name, and do it with the least amount of surrender possible.

All this was complicated by another situation that put a twelve-century yoke around quality control in the church, namely, government recognition of the church, beginning with Constantine. The legal equation that "citizen" equalled "Christian" anywhere in the empire placed a complete squelch on the church's having meaningful membership standards. Therefore, any possibility that the church could be a disciplined community as a whole was completely lost. Since entrance standards could not be established, there soon developed the sacrament of penance, an imposed attempt to control the life of the church, but since the ruling powers were in the hands of the state, this piece of machinery became more and more an instrument of secular power for both bishop and king.

Looking back, we have to acknowledge that the Holy Spirit has always loved his church and worked in it and with it to his glory. There were still, and have always been, those Christian servants who yearned for the purity of the witness of the church. Since the community as a whole was really nothing more than a secular society with a pious label, the only sincere answer was the development of disciplined and dedicated communities within the church. These had two primary characteristics: (a) they could prescribe their own high regimen for membership, which was a process of filtering out the insincere or unprepared, and (b) they were function-oriented—being either active, such as missionaries, teachers, preachers, and later the manpower for hospitals, schools, social service movements, etc., or contemplative, such as prayer orders, scholars, theologians, etc. I submit that if this second level of asceticism had not been born, the church as the identifiable body of Christ would not have survived.

You might say that it was a movement of churches, separate in discipline and function, yet manifesting a medieval ecumenicity in a common loyalty to the Holy See.

Look at the twelfth and thirteenth centuries, known as the age of the cathedrals. Roland Bainton correctly points out that this was a time of high order, when the influence of the church was saturating Europe and stimulating society to raise its high stone towers over the cities. As Christ had said, "And I, if I be lifted up . . . , will draw all men unto me." The development of church structure really came about by the extraordinary effectiveness of the several orders, doing their complicated tasks with a cumulative organizational integrity, showing the world that the church really takes its business seriously. The writings of Thomas Aquinas, frequently called collectively the Great Resolution, climax and summarize the devotion of that age, capsulizing the insights of communities of total dedication. And this is the baby that the Reformation threw out with the bath when it proclaimed too loudly the misleading catchphrase, "The priesthood of all believers."

But the basic spirit of special preparation for special goals could not be destroyed. Protestantism has had its succession of unofficial holy orders, such as Bible societies, temperance leagues, Masonic orders, and in the 1960's, the civil rights movement. Though it can't be said that these were produced *by* the church, and supported *by* it totally, it can be said that they were born *in* the church and reflect that birth. The civil rights fellowship receives support and encouragement from that slice of the church across the country that sees and agrees and is willing to stand with the workers and give for them. It may not be *the* church that is demonstrating, witnessing, going to jail, pleading the cause with warm bodies on the spot; it can be said that it is a certain concerned portion of the church that is doing this in Christ's name. In a way they represent us in that they are motivated by their commitment to Christian values, and in a way they don't represent us, because given the same challenge we might choose a different path of action.

All of which leads me to predict the development of a new constellation of holy orders. In the sense in which I use the term, an order is a regulated community disciplined by its common agreements, *within* the church, under the direction and approval of the courts of the church, dedicated to loyal and effective purposes in *certain* fields.

The first line of evidence—beginning of course at Taizé where the medieval pattern is most closely followed, going from there to Iona and then to the lay institutes of continental Europe and the group fellowship movements in this country such as Kirkridge, Order of the Yoke, and Camp Farthest Out—shows that there is a strong desire to deepen the too-shallow standards of the contemporary church and to unite in mutually supportive, even judgmental, communities of purpose.

The second line of evidence is more along functional than organizational lines but is no less apparent. Ordained ministers are really a rather select holy order, with strong preparatory requirements such as the ordeal of seminary, and ordination examinations. Within this classification, clergymen break up into subgroups, some of them engaged in prayer fellowships, study circles, social action, or the administration of ecclesiastical mechanics. Each of these serves a purpose, probably more than is visible. They serve to give strength and vitality to the mutual convictions and clarification of our witness.

Beyond the ordained clergy are associations of Christian educators, church music directors and organists, church administrators. As the crisis of survival intensifies, these groups will tighten their standards.

You might say that these are not holy orders at all, rather new kinds of guilds, or pious labor unions, and I agree. But they will become holy orders, because they have to. They will become more select, more demanding of quality, and eventually will impose some order of discipline upon their participants. Even now, the Hattiesburg Ministers Project and the Delta Ministry, under the aegis of the National Council of Churches, exact a regimen for their participants of poverty, chastity, and obedience, which even though temporary is absolutely necessary to meet the needs of the times. The achievement of any function requires a preparation equal to the severity of the function. As we discover we have enormous tasks to do, we will gather those Christians concerned about each cause, and equip them for their tasks.

The church soon discovered that great accomplishments cost heavily. To pay the price, the ascetic life had to become austere. So will it have to be today. The church also discovered that the community setting, in which persons with similar concerns give one another partnership and support, was both traditional and effective.

Let's look at those vows again: poverty, chastity, obedience. In the twentieth century, a vow of poverty may mean the replacement of the Protestant acquisition ethic, in which the main goal in life is financial security, with the acceptance of a simple standard of living and a goal of service. It may mean the decision to share this world's goods with needy society or some particular project of the church. It may mean the denial of promotions at work to continue effectiveness at a lower level. The funeral procession of Martin Luther King, Jr., in which his body was carried through the streets of Atlanta in a mule wagon followed by 100,000 mourners, may be the apocalyptic emblem of the church's respect for the impoverished, and a vow to share the poverty.

The vow of chastity can mean celibacy, but in the Protestant context it can mean other things too. It could mean, for instance, that a certain couple agree to remain childless for specified years of service or for their lifetime if the circumstances of their order call for it. It could mean the postponement of marriage during a novitiate or training period. Probably its principal meaning would be the vow to remain sexually honest and represent under all conditions the Christian reverence for the mating act in a world in which sexual symbolism is pretty confused. And that may be a bigger discipline than abstinence.

The vow of obedience in the modern holy order does not eliminate dialogue, but it does mean that a community's decisions must be taken seriously and put before individual opinion.

For example, I believe that in these times there is no justification whatever for a church-related hospital until we develop a disciplined holy order of Christian healers, to equal and surpass the orders that operate the present Roman Catholic hospitals. Someday, somewhere, there is going to be an articulate and dedicated Christian who will move to orient his faith to the healing arts, as did Dr. Tom Dooley. He may be a doctor, or administrator, or ambulance driver, or whatever. He will gather a few other highly motivated Christians about him. Agreeing upon some very basic rules of devotion, life, behavior, and commitment, and gaining the cooperation of some institution, they will put aside the priorities of the ordinary life to serve in witness. This holy order may wind up being uniquely vocational, it's membership being, for example, all orderlies, or nurses, or janitors, or bedpan cleaners. Whatever it is, it will inject into the life of the hospital just enough of the flavor of Christian concern in sacrifice that that particular hospital can offer something more than custodially and scientifically excellent care. The present practice of having a professional chaplain on the premises of a hospital shows that we really yearn to do this very thing, but without disciplined and obedient troops that resemble nothing else in this world, our church-related hospitals are really nothing more than carbon copies of other hospitals.

Indeed, the movement may already be farther under way than we suspect. An article in the April 22, 1958, *New York Times* titled "Catholic Underground Churches Grow" tells of clandestine groups that meet without the endorsement of the bishop and style themselves as equivalents of the "free universities." The article quotes a journalist layman who predicts that "people who want to be part of a Christian community will have the option of going either to a traditional parish church or joining a smaller, more intimate free church." Although these groups, estimated at several hundred, vary widely in the form they take, almost all include new liturgical experimentation, a concern for social action, and radical questionings of traditional church teachings. Discussions tend to deal with fundamental questions such as, How is it possible to be a Christian in a secular world?

How terribly desperate we are for an order of married nonparents who are willing to live in the destitution of the inner city and befriend the human garbage that now only paid social workers and storefront revival centers will touch! Consider ministry to the elderly, the handicapped, the ex-convicts, newly arrived immigrants, and on and on!

Finally, the mandate to stay on the firing line calls for

an unveiling of the word "witness." Perhaps the use of the word "martyr" is overcolored by drama, sentiment, and the embellishment of time. Nonetheless, the everyday, ordinary function of "witnessing" very early proved to be an enormously expensive operation. In Roman jurisprudence, which had no bill of rights, to testify to an accusation or defense was to lay oneself wide open to the wrath of the magistrate, the hostility of the public, or corrective exile or slavery. So be it. To be a witness is to attest to the truth, and the fabric of faith requires it.

This brings attention not so much to the doing, the witnessing, the martyring if you please, but to the subject being affirmed. A Negro bears witness to everyone who sees him that he is a black man; it is the apparent fact of his nature. It isn't what he does that makes this evident; it's what he *is*. Similarly, a truthful witness on the stand or in the marketplace has become a witness not by what he does but by the undeniable reality of what he tells of. This is the way the early church saw it. Christ was the fulfillment of the Messianic destiny, and all human life was affected by it. For a disciple, then, all life was simply a testimony that that was true. Since there was absolutely nothing to be done about it but to witness to it, the early Christians (or some of them, at least) found no alternative but to pay the price—banishment, imprisonment, slavery, death. That's why we call them "martyrs," witnesses.

Things haven't really changed all that much. The church today still is moved by the completeness of the divine revelation in Christ—whatever that may mean in the atomic-age context. As a matter of fact, the channels of witness are much more numerous and available now than then. There is, for instance, the witness of having concerns that transcend the local scene. A person who has never been troubled by want witnesses when he is concerned about the hungry. A person who basks in the free discourse of a democratic society shows allegiance to higher things when he is mindful of other people's tyranny. A Christian makes a wee bit more humane the big cold world when he gives time and money to assuage the loneliness of others. This is elementary witness.

But in many places, many people of goodwill outshine the Christians in their humanity. The difference for the believer is the *call to ultimacy*, to go the whole way as Christ did for us. It's the only real witness and the totality of our destiny. One definition of love is that quality in a person that guarantees he'll never desert. The effective witness of the church is the measure of sticking it out to the very last. That's why the book of Revelation can *under no circumstances* be interpreted as a passport to an easier world. It symbolically reflects the gospel that it is our glory to stick it out. In a recent movie about the sinking of the *Titanic*, there are many touching scenes of devoted self-sacrifice so that loved ones, or young ones, or innocent ones can live. Charles Dickens may have been tediously Victorian in *A Tale of Two Cities*, but Sidney Carton epitomizes the only kind of love that will honestly make the Messianic age known to sinful men.

How does the church lay itself on the block today? After the spending of resources, and the transcending of nonultimate concerns, and the gathering into determined task forces, what's left? Just the whole ball of wax, that's all. Take the agonies of racial injustice. Any wise man knows that the foundations of this horror root very deeply in the collective personality of man. No particular tactic, whether it be a housing breakthrough, a civil rights bill, or an integrated city, is going to be much of a solution. The problem is a sickness deeper than that. Decades, perhaps centuries, of confusion, frustration, uncertainty, and incredibly complex problems lie ahead. Witness means being in there trying, involved with every movement of meaning, being susceptible to error, exposed to accusation, accepting our own shallowness. Those of us who are white may find ourselves blocked at every turn from any sense of achievement, indeed being the very objects of the resentful hostility that must needs come out. What appears to be the right direction, or *a* right direction, or just *hopefully* a right direction must be our way until proven otherwise. And we must stand responsible for the consequences of being wrong; and after a hundred times around, finding ourselves right back where we started but spent and resourceless, we start again. That, in our day, is one meaning of the cross, though much less dramatic in appearance. In fact, the cross is only authentic when all vestiges of what may look like heroism are gone.

Consider the frightened, defensive people who comprise the extreme right, the fundamentalists, the John Birchers, the KKK. Scorn comes easy to knowledgeable society as it beholds the unethical obstructionism used by the ultraconservatives. Yet scorn is itself a form of defense, and seldom does it pay the big price that reconciles. People will only come crawling out of their hiding places when there is nothing to be afraid of. The reconciling ministry of these days is going to take and take and take the paranoid accusations and respond in some way that affirms the beloved humanity of the accusers—even if division and destruction of precious programs and institutions are part of it. And again at the end, there will be no record of heroism—just reconciliation, whose glory belongs to God.

We look not too far ahead to a rather drastic realignment of the centers of power in this world. The white European-American clique has had its day, and men of other colors and cultures will be directing the big developments someday. When that day comes, the witness of a church willing to exalt all men will be remembered not for its heroism, but simply because it was the right thing to do. Our sentimental missionary stories about brown eyes filled with tears of gratitude because of the noble paternalism of rich white brothers are far more harmful than helpful. We don't want the Christians of the Congo to be eternally in our debt, or even especially grateful because we did so much for them. We just want them to know the gospel, and be free to witness to it in their way, and be free to forget who brought it. This is precisely the tone of Paul's admonition to the Corinthian church to forget their particular apostolic heroes and be of the same mind. "For Christ did not send me to baptize but to preach the gospel, and not with eloquent wisdom, lest the cross of Christ be emptied of its power." (I Cor. 1:17.)

The cross means that although there are some few dramatic times when we get to see a reconciling result of our lives, the vast bulk of our witness will have its effects, if any, far beyond our recognition. The particular pro-African, procommunist, and value-threatening attitudes of an Nkrumah or a Castro may be a dismaying shock to traditional Christians but can probably be traced in motive and power directly to the nineteenth-century missions and may further be a genuine transitional step to a new Africa or Cuba that does indeed fulfill a portion of the Christian dream. When that fulfillment comes about, there will be no thank-you or historical footnotes. So be it. It had to happen that way. If the Black Power movement in America, now so uneasily watched by a threatened white majority, does indeed liberate some new social reforms, we could probably note among ourselves that the strong Protestant Christian influence among Negroes surfaced at the right time. But the self-assurance is unnecessary and shallow. Verily, we have our reward.

The price that is yet to be paid for the world at peace, that immeasurably gigantic sacrifice to be made by *somebody,* could be for us an investment in faith. War is caused by poverty, and we follow the one who for our sakes became poor. A thousand directions await us, and a million lives could be poured out before a small reconciling progress is noted. Laws, taxes, aid programs, Peace Corps projects, industrial replanning, lobbying for different foreign policies, hundreds of man-years in ghettos and barrennesses, all comprise a very small down payment. To offer these a thousand times over is only to start. We still have the call to pay it all, the ultimate. And if we go bankrupt before the victory, we cannot rest in exhausted masochism, but ever must wonder if it was the right way. The cross is often the misery of confused ambivalence.

War is caused by sick and tyranical political systems. We know only too well that a beautifully constructed constitution is only a piece of paper, that something far stronger in the nature of a climate of confidence and responsibility brings health to a balanced government. We have yet to study the ashes of the Third Reich to see where individual human relationships began their deterioration that produced a collective monster. Those of us Christians who live in the U.S.A. or England could well assess the price now required in the way of societal integrity to counteract the same trends here. Why did the camel's-nose-in-the-tent entanglement in Vietnam even get started? Are there Christians on the thousands of little I-Thou frontiers sticking it out to prevent others, to prevent a U.S.A., from becoming infected with a fatal dehumanizing corrosion? When a war does not occur, who knows what we missed? Who gets the credit? Who cares? Reconciliation is frequently marked by the absence of dramatic tragedy, which means that nobody saw. Praise God.

What about the shallow, provincial, self-satisfied nature of American middle-class suburban life? What about the big wide cracks of mediocrity, loneliness, alienation, into which so many of us fall as casualties? Does this need a reconciling ministry? There seems to be a great open blank when it comes to understanding the sacrificial nature of marriage, the excruciating demands of honest interpersonal relationships, the meaningfulness of morality. And do great lamentations or pontifical pronouncements make much difference? Here too the complete reservoir of love and commitment of the Christian church could be absorbed by Wednesday of next week with little evident result. But perhaps it ought to, and bear its own witness. After all, Christ gave all he had in less than three years. The ways of going about it aren't terribly mysterious. Everybody lives next door to a domestic tragedy that needs the loving concern of an amateur. Churches have resources to set up counseling services, to support community social service organizations, to grant scholarships, to dialogue honestly with the social sciences, to create or maintain or affect institutions and programs, to be authentically human. Church people don't have answers; they have pretty much the same diseases themselves. They just have a reason to be hopeful, and that hopefulness gives for an openness to uncritical listening and unpretentious response. Actually, nearly everything needed to be said is being said, all the way from Albee and Arthur Miller to Peanuts. Good grief, Charlie Brown! Why not just fill in the cracks? With ourselves, as fellow human beings.

Why dream of another world when there is so much downright relevant belongingness to the gospel right here? "Blessed are those who are invited to the marriage supper of the Lamb." (Rev. 19:9.) It's our holy calling to stick it out.

6

The Holy City

As the writer of Ecclesiastes so aptly said, there's a time for everything. He philosophizes about a time to be born and a time to die, to kill and to heal, to break down and to build up, to love and to hate. The writer of the Apocalypse agrees thoroughly, and in the throes of dealing with the time to face the world in courage, he says there is also a time to dream in faith.

This last book of the Bible follows a very clear and understandable process in picking up the bruised Christians of the day and setting them in responsible motion. It's not especially logical, but it is very much the way the healing human spirit goes. For after assessing the imperfect church, the harsh facts of this world, the mysterious durability of the community of faithfulness, and the presence of Christ among his own, he, John, knows with all men of feeling that it is a time to look ahead to the sum of it all.

Not a convincing argument for the bolstering up of the morale but rather a spirit-lifting blaze of trumpets in affirming finale, the resonant acclamations say more to the hearing souls than any chain of logic ever could. In the blazing pictures of the fulfilled promises at the end of

Revelation, the Christian church is put squarely in the tradition of the fathers. For the Bible is a succession of pilgrimage stories, a little community going from an old and unsatisfactory confinement toward a new life: Abraham going out from Ur "not knowing whither he went" to a new land, Joseph's brothers leaving behind a famine to go to Egypt, the children of Israel escaping from slavery to a land "flowing with milk and honey," Ezra going home to Jerusalem, and finally at Jesus' pastoral encouragement, the Christians pointing their lives toward the Kingdom of God.

The last four chapters of the Apocalypse are among the most sublime passages in all poesy. Properly so, for they sum up in undisguised rapture the whole apex of Christian hope, bringing together the three heretofore separate "awaited events" that the little group yearned for so intensely: the coming victory, the supremacy of love and justice over evil, and the miracle of resurrection.

But how to put these great assurances into words? How possibly can the message be imparted to such desperate, simple-minded, hurt, and trusting people? For the writer, the answer to this is clear. Tick off all the folk symbols of deepest meaning, in accumulating crescendo of emotional impact, and leave them with an *enduring impression* that what they trust is eternally trustworthy. And if God has led the messenger in his preparation of the message, he will help those who hear to see it through in a confidence stronger than chains.

In point of fact, the formula is the same for us. Some years ago, a cartoon appeared in the *Saturday Review*, showing two tourists riding camels by the Sphinx. One says, "I wonder, if he could speak, what he'd say?" The other replies, "I'd be happy if he'd just tell me it's a good world." In spite of our great sophistication about the scientific details of our universe, the one thing we really need in order to be able to face tomorrow responsibly is the simple assurance from *some* authoritative source that it's a good world. Whether we be in formal seminar on the campus, instructing our children by the hearth, or crying out alone in the night, the need is always the same. O God, make tomorrow worth something, not just another spasm of futility. Let it lead *somewhere* that man may be thankful!

So John of Patmos speaks to us. Or at least, to me. He speaks pictorially but assuringly of what it all leads to for the Christian, and he gives us something to dream about where dreaming makes us understand the present and await the future expectantly. Like a skillful composer who calls up themes we've heard before, but in a new key and a new tempo and a brilliant cadence, the poet now rings some old themes in a way that brightens our hearing.

The White Horse (Rev. 19:11-16). A familiar figure rides back into our vision, the symbol of aggressive, creative, capable, libidinous *man.* We've seen him before. But now we know more than we knew before about what we're up against; and after outlasting our own fright and reticence and pessimism, we see man in a new light, which is the only real way to start. The ideal society is still going to be made up of people, by and large the selfsame people we associate with now. The very ones who annoy us on the freeway and jostle us on the subway, with their drives for comfort, security, and ego-fulfillment, are to be our fellow citizens in the Promised Land. This is what Jesus meant when responding to the message that his family was waiting for him. "Who are my mother and my brothers?" he asked, and then waving to all who stood around, "*You* are my mother and my brothers!" (Matt. 12:48, 49).

141

We saw the white horse before, indeed, as the first of a long list of realities that could either frighten us or challenge us. Now we start again at the same place, but we are describing goals rather than surveying the raw material. So both the reality and the dream have to do with that undefinable vitality in man that so mysteriously resembles both God and the animals. The difference here is that we are brought to see the white rider using his sword as the word of truth in a new commitment to virtue. It is a newly directed humanity.

In his recent encyclical, "On the Development of Peoples," Pope Paul VI wrote: "What must be aimed at is complete humanism . . . , the fully rounded development of the whole man and of all men." Right! All the knotty problems that bedevil us and distort us into a sick society are the symptoms of our *in*complete humanism.

Racism, as uncovered by commissions, dramatized in demonstrations, and bemoaned by all colors, is a result of our unwillingness to be completely human. James Baldwin is quite right when he points out that it's not just the problem of the Negro's gaining acceptance by the white man, but much more it is that the white man deeply needs the Negro as a co-human before he can realize his own humanity. He who does not sense the richness of the unity of mankind misses the unity of a man. Whatever it is that is yet to happen in the cities and migrant labor areas, on Indian reservations and in South Africa, has a potential, according to this special vision, of revealing to us man as we never really knew him. The Christian conscience and the humanitarian's dream stir us to yearn.

Yes, yearn we do. A psychiatrist studying the popularity of the use of LSD, the "mind-blowing" drug, theorizes that the motive for taking LSD is essentially the same as for religion. It is thought to be one way of clearing away distractions and becoming fully and pleasantly *aware*, that is, human. That this would even be a theory shows that this doctor feels every person has a deep and perhaps unconscious drive to realize his full humanness. The use of hallucinatory drugs may be a poorly advised way to go about it, but the purpose is still revealing of personality.

The same may also be said about the symbols of sex in this rather erotically saturated time. It may be that the curiosity that sells so many "candid" novels and encourages the four-letter vocabulary and seems to promote extramarital liaisons is really not so prurient after all. It may, as a matter of fact, be the amoral quest for the confirmation of a realized humanity, with all the morality that discovery may bring. What the white horse holds before us as a goal worth hoping for is a humanity that understands its own finiteness and accepts its lot with a measure of faith in dealing with the truth, the Word of God. The other realities, the inevitables of death and war and economic necessity, are rather static in redemptive possibility; but that life juice that drives us all to want to prevail, with God's help, *that* could be something! Or, at least, it could give us cause for hope.

Presumptuously, I would translate this passage (Rev. 19:11-16) into the language most meaningful to my twentieth-century mind:

Then I saw things in a new light,
And there was *man*, the same man I had always known,
But now a new and different mankind;
For this man had made a decision
Down deep
To see me, his fellow, in my true heritage
Of holiness.
And he really longed to honor and be honored,

143

As Christ honored him.
And he was a leader of men.

The Great Supper (*Rev. 19:17-18*). "Come to the great banquet of God!" Lo and behold, a part of the dream of the future is a party right now! Completely in accord with the whole Hebrew-Christian tradition, the gathering of the family, or tribe, or community for a shared festival meal is an appropriate scene in any Christian's dream of the way God works things out. Notice how the central enactments of God's unusual grace were born under duress. The Passover, undoubtedly the oldest continuing ritual of freedom and thanksgiving, celebrates the beginning of the slaves' rebellion with all its anxiety and stress. The Christian Eucharist, or communion service, or Mass, or Lord's Supper, commemorates the end of an earthly ministry and the beginning of mortal tribulation. Quite consistently, then, as this pastoral leader, John, is suggesting what our minds could dwell on in troublous times, he proposes the symbol of a big feast.

And why not? Joy, deep joy, is the root of the Christian's outlook on life. So when the real issues begin to collide in some kind of ultimate showdown, it is most appropriate for the believers to whoop it up. "The astonishing thing about the Christian faith," writes none other than Harvey G. Cox, "is that it insists on being joyful even during times and occasions when most people feel that joy is an inappropriate emotion. One only has to remember the fact that jazz had its origin in the Negro funerals of New Orleans." There is no kind of completely blind alley in which there are not possibilities for life that give cause for joy.

Notice the New Testament point to joy. Whereas John the Baptist came fasting, Jesus came feasting, "living it up" with Pharisee and outcast alike. His life was a constant celebration of the things that are *really* true, the things more important than all the dreary sordidness this world can produce. When he laid eyes on lepers covered with repulsive sores and seen by others as less than human, Jesus celebrated their nobility in healing and respect. When he beheld the tragedy of a mixed-up harlot who had lost all sense of wholeness, he and she had a party at the well from which she came with a new sense of reverence and forgiveness.

This vision of the great banquet, then, is a sample of the way the Christian celebrates the inevitable with his brothers. A father of young children, told that he has incurable leukemia, turns to his wife with a smile, "We'll just have time to get that trip to Hawaii in." In prison, with a sentence of death upon his head, Dietrich Bonhoeffer celebrates the Eucharist ("the holy thanksgiving"), as have so many others through the years, in league with his fellow prisoners. Now, living in an apocalyptic time, with God-knows-what about to happen, what is there to do? Celebrate! Look on the world, as John Wesley looked on the poor of his day, "hopefully." Look on the hostile explosions in the ghettos and rejoice together that men are responding to the invitation to yearn for a better life. Offer yourself, of course, as whatever it may take to heal, but rejoice meanwhile that there even is a struggle, for in it there is a spirit of truth that may, through God's grace, touch man redemptively.

It is the unpredictable lightninglike nature of the Holy Spirit that we celebrate. No matter what rods, devices, plans, dreams, or directions we may put in his way, he will strike where he will. Whatever our prophecies of doom, he knows more about it than we do. When the Norman host overran England in 1066, a Welsh bishop predicted that the untold savagery of the pagan Gauls would drive every bit of Christian morality from the "sceptred isle." He was just as wrong as the church leader of Carthage who, seeing the oncoming Muslim hordes, calmed his people by saying that God would not permit such infidels to prevail in North Africa. In either case, the good priests would have done well to gather their people in glad recognition that God knows what he is doing.

This is the answer he always gives when we raise our anxious questions: "Celebrate." And the faithful response is to do just that, and to do it as Cox suggests, "within the ambience of a loving mystery which is at the core of all human existence." Suppose the very worst should happen —defeat by the Commies, or destruction by the bomb, or disease, or death, or idiot's stupor. The Very Most is more true, meaningful, and enduring than the very worst. Face the world with that!

When I read this passage (Rev. 19:17-18), I restate it to myself:

> Then it occurred to me that the most honest way
> To live in the slipstream of that powerful
> Healing spirit
> Was simply to accept God's invitation to trust,
> To see his victorious presence
> In the eyes of my fellow trusters,
> In the little glimpses of splendor in
> Occasional incidents of
> Love,
> Justice,
> Human care,
> To share the fact that I trust by living
> Unashamedly human,
> And to enjoy it!

The Thousand-Year Exile (Rev. 20:2-7). Wouldn't you think that any dream of a "happy issue out of all our afflictions" would do away with the villain completely? After all, if you're going to dream, go all the way! But here the dragon, the dissident element in the life of man, is only put on "hold" for a thousand years, after which "he must be loosed for a little while" (Rev. 20:3). It's another way of saying, dear friends, that human existence will never be completely free of that old dragon, that symbol of all that is demonic and beastly about my enemy, my neighbor, myself. He may go through times of repression, but it seems to be a part of the divine design that moral conflict is a part of the definition of you and me.

Interestingly enough, this is also the discovery of those who would like to eliminate the "childish superstition" of religion as a means of building the ideal society. Just as we are told that the dragon will always be with us, so are the Communists now discovering that Christianity has the same stubborn deeper-than-we-thought intrinsic durability. Writes Peter Grose in *The New York Times:* "Fifty years of Communist rule has not killed religion, and the commissars cannot figure out why."

Everything seems clear in the Marxist texts, he points out. The official philosophy has demonstrated that as man's intellectual and scientific awareness grows, his need for faith in a "God in the unfathomable beyond" should fade away. "That is what ought to happen," Grose quotes a Soviet official, "but I must admit it's doing it very slowly."

Sound familiar? We've been saying the same thing, on the other side of the coin, for centuries. When man hears the gospel, he should hear it gladly and work for a world that reflects this amazing news. At least, that is what ought to happen, but we must admit . . .

The fact of the matter is that we all continue to underestimate the profound rooting in all of us that both good and evil have. David Roberts' book title *The Grandeur and Misery of Man* tells the directions of insight we need to know about ourselves. There are times when our near-sightedness is more in one direction than the other, as in times of naïve overoptimism, such as the late Victorian age, or of oppressive gloom, as the immediate post-World War II time.

The important thing for Christians in unusually de-manding times is to avoid self-deception. Notice that this caution comes in the drama immediately following the great banquet. Remember also that in the stories of both Passover and the Last Supper, the greatest tribulation came after the table. Feasting is no time to be lulled into a gorged stupor that incapacitates us for life. Rather it is the time of preparation—courage for the spirit and nour-ishment for the body—for the real fight that is yet to come. So it is that even though the dragon is going to be muz-zled for a goodly time, he'll be back. And even when he's out of sight, brother, he's not dead yet.

It is the story of marriage. When courtship has achieved its sweet goal, the happy pair has covenanted together and the new home started, the real drama of human pos-sibility and tragedy has only begun. The dragon of lone-liness and single incompletion that the premarital soul tries so hard to conquer has not been entirely accounted for. "There is no relationship of any kind," said a mar-riage counselor recently, "more dangerous than family life. Here can be some of the deepest satisfactions and at the same time the most painful and destructive hurts that are ever experienced."

One remembers the stories of utopian communities founded by highly motivated people determining to leave the worst behind and provide for a new order free from the tiresome and troublous ways. The Mayflower Compact and the struggling little Plymouth community sought a new kind of religious freedom and developed a theocratic tyranny more despotic than ever. The Congo broke from Belgium (as a hundred colonies have slashed the umbilical cords of empire) to seek a new dignity and promptly immersed itself in a bloodbath. The Mormons went a thousand miles into the unwanted desert to found a new Zion where God's people could be themselves, but Salt Lake City today has the same proportion of human miseries as any other city. The old dragon is only serving a light sentence in the city jail, and on a still night you can hear his grumblings clear to the suburbs.

But at least, he *is* in trouble. Look again at the condition of religion in Russia. Curiosity has replaced hostility toward religion in the present Soviet generation. The reason is not difficult to determine. A constant theme of modern Soviet writing is the individual's lack of a sense of purpose in today's society, the old Russian theme of nihilism. Building for the human mind and body, the Communists have ignored the human soul.

Kornei I. Chukovsky, a writer who is now preparing an edition of Bible stories for Russian young people, tells of overhearing this conversation one day in a Moscow park: "Is there a God?" asked one boy of seven years or so. "We Communists don't believe so," his slightly older playmate said confidently, "but of course, maybe he does exist anyway."

What the dragon stands for and what the Lamb means to us are both permanent fixtures and we might as well reckon with both, trusting in the eventual victory of our Lord and of his Christ.

An updated reflection on this passage (Rev. 20:1-7) comes to me in this wise:

And I rehearsed in my soul that warfare
So consuming,
My own moral schizophrenia,
That same despairing mystery that every
Morning newspaper tells from everywhere,
But this time I saw that the corruption
I had always thought to be despairingly strong,
Was weak!
Vulnerable!
It wasn't destined by the gods to prevail!
It could be assailed, restrained.
I did not find, however, that it was
Mortal.
Just not inevitably victorious.
But that was enough for me.

The Dwelling of God Is with Men (*Rev. 21:1-4*). Now comes the most sublime, assuring, realistic, judgmental directive of the whole Christian literature. A whole new order inserts itself into our sphere "coming down out of heaven."

"I have a dream!" shouted Martin Luther King, Jr., on the steps of the Lincoln Memorial. And only a day and a half before his violent death he told an audience: "I would like to live a long life. . . . But I'm not concerned about that now. . . . *I've seen the Promised Land!*" History will affirm that his assassination only elaborated the splendor of that dream. He didn't need to elaborate on that dream, either; ten million black Americans knew what it was viscerally enough to have their hearts quickened. What he proclaimed was just too appropriately an extension of what he had been living for to die with him.

His dream was one of the great visions of history because of its simplicity and beauty. It was a dream of a society of justice and love. It was, in fact, the twentieth-century Negro's perspective on the Holy City that John of

Patmos saw. No, don't try to transpose this vision to some far-off, sometime, somewhere-else kind of dream. The text becomes quite unambiguous in its prepositions— "down" when talking of the direction of this new order, and "with" when saying where God dwells. This Holy City proposition is the reality in which Christians live here and now. King wasn't saying that Negroes should abide with the injustice and degradation of the present time because someday they would be translated to another world where things were different. He didn't organize marches in the streets of modern Babylons to witness to the futility of it all here. His vision was that of the newness of the Holy City being reflected, in imperfect fragments perhaps but still in evidence, where people live.

Those promises, those golden assuring promises, that God will dwell where men hurt, and heal them, and dry their tears, and take from them the tragedies of lostness and death, are the daily paychecks of hope. In a certain sense, King himself was an incarnate fulfillment of the promise, as is the life of any man possessed by love and dedication. Such promises *do* exist, here and now, and in our language, and in our realm of experience. "It was King," writes Peter Schrag in the *Saturday Review* (April 20, 1968, p. 28), "who took the cadences and images of the Baptist preacher, traditionally directed to the hereafter, and applied them to the present. For him, the promised land was not an exit from this world but an entrance, a rap on the locked shutters of the national conscience."

What Christians cannot forget in their wildest dreamings, and what God affirms to us in Christ, is the humanness of humanity, the flesh-and-blood-and-gristle creation that he designed as the setting for the Holy City to have its regnancy.

It puts on every Christian's eyes a very special kind of glasses that causes him to see, when he looks at the world around him, things that without faith he would miss. The Christian looks at the jungles of Vietnam, and where the American public sees little brown men with subhuman lives and demonic, violent terror threatening "civilization," he is "constrained by love" to see the same humanity we taste, in a slightly different kind of package. There are to be found the same kinds of yearnings, ideals, needs for recognition and love, strengths of character and reflections of compassion, struggling desperately for an expression that makes way for honor and trust. The Christian walks the streets of busy commerce and depressed slums, always reminded that God calls us to an order of holiness, and that he gave his Son that all men—derelicts, criminals, corporation presidents, shop clerks, and pickpockets—may somehow sense the all-important reality of forgiveness and acceptance.

That this is always seen in the terms of the local circumstances is God's doing, not an annoying happenstance. Charles Davis maintains that "men can come to Christ only from within their human situation. . . . Every formulation of Christian belief belongs to a particular historical context and represents a limited understanding from a given standpoint. Standpoints change, and the believer must constantly review the formulations he has inherited in the light of a fresh understanding." (*A Question of Conscience,* p. 21.)

Does this mean that the vision of the Holy City has to be modified, diluted? Not at all. The assurance is given to us as the order that is most true, always true. God's place *is* with men, and whatever the situation is, however oppressive the inhumanity and degrading injustice, the

Promised Land is always in the condition of unfolding, appearing, more relevant than the blight. The Christian never accepts the present conditions as the final word, because the only real finality is the Kingdom of God, and he has seen it. Not clearly, not perfectly, not even enough to understand it, but he has seen that kind of glimpse in Christ that makes the Kingdom his lifelong obsession.

These words are being written only a few paces away from the campus of a mighty university where at this minute a rebellion is under way, with a large group of students holding the administration in siege. The issue, according to the student leaders, many of whom would quickly disclaim any kind of religious idealism, is a moral one. It involves the institution's use of a nearby park for a new building, the park really belonging, the vocal students claim, to the poor people nearby. Whether their judgment is a little too purist or simplistic and whether the whole flap is really on this subject or just reflective of the confused restiveness of our times none of us can now say. It does show, however, that all of us have a need to have a worthy dream, and an outsize compulsion to be obedient to that dream. There are inner voices that all generations, but especially the younger generation, can only repress at great damage to their self-image.

These same motives were with the early Christians, as they were with the Romans and the folk of all times. Ours has been an amazingly enduring dream. Francis of Assisi, a thousand years after the catacombs, faced the Muslim sultan in his tent with it, John Bunyan languished "in durance vile" and wrote about it, John Calvin systematically lived for it, and Martin Luther King, Jr., died for it, and it's all the same dream. The picture of the Holy City in the book of Revelation (Rev. 21:1-4) is the portrayal of an order of society where God's sovereignty is known and humanity discovers its fullest destiny, in love and justice.

> Then it seemed to me that this whole
> Disordered, painful, diseased world
> Began to make sense.
> God has put into it the foretaste
> Of the way things are really meant to be.
> Even more, he occupies it with us;
> There is a splendor about love
> And genuine selfless concern
> And a community of understanding
> Acceptance
> That is his splendor.
> I can look for it everywhere; it is.
> I can expect it anywhere.
> I can wait for it forever.

The City Foursquare (*Rev. 21:15-21*). A city whose measurements are exactly even and symmetrical and whose elements are precious materials is of course the picture of an ordered society that is secure, dependable, and just. This is of course the dream not only of the Christian but of every responsible, socially sensitive person. These are to be found in every tradition, and at this point the longings of all different kinds of people and philosophies converge into one simple but beautiful picture. The legalist, either Pharisee of old or jurist of today, yearns for such a dream, as does the most far-out hippie, or anarchist, or even Communist. After all, there are two places where all humanity confesses its commonality, the grave and the dream of justice.

It may appear to some as though there are opposite schools in interpretation of Revelation and that between them exists an irreconcilable conflict. The camps that differ so widely put the chasm of division on the basis of "future" or "present," with many subdivisions in each column. The Biblical literalism in which I was raised not only taught that every event depicted in the Apocalypse was yet to be realized but that there were enough clues in the text to work out a possible timetable, leaving this picture of the Holy City and its glistening purity to come either at the end of history or in a completely other arena of timelessness and spacelessness. It may seem surprising for me to say that that viewpoint is totally acceptable to me. For, since the book is written as an instrument to quicken our faith and give reason for our hope, and since its symbols are so profoundly touching to the human heart, any way of receiving it that does indeed cause glad hallelujahs to spring from the believer's heart reflects the authenticity of the book. I have written not from the viewpoint of the archaeologist-scholar-historian, but as a responder.

I knew nothing at all about Beethoven, his manner of composing, or even the school he represented. But one day, in church, I heard the organist play as a prelude the second movement from the popular Fifth Symphony. And as that gentle, insistent, glad, positive melody floated from those pipes, something inside my emotional response center wanted to cry out a loud Yes! That day the sun was a little brighter, relationships a bit more secure, and a particular adolescent confusion turned into an affirmation. Since that time, I have learned many of the details about the symphony, even stood in the room in Vienna where the crotchety, lonely man worked on it through a bitter cold winter. It's all been very interesting and enlightening but hasn't changed the effect, the response, the golden touch on my soul of that first hearing.

Just so with the elaborate visions of this book. I heard

them first in an atmosphere of rock-ribbed fundamental-ism, preached in fiery and world-denying rhetoric but coming across in a dream of singular and breathtaking assurances that hope, and faithfulness, and unashamed idealism were all worth pinning one's life on. The discoveries about the Christian faith and story, and the scholar's additional information about Revelation have all only made those original impressions all the deeper and the gratitude for having heard them more intense.

Dr. Louis Talbot, then pastor of the Church of the Open Door in Los Angeles, used to say that the whole core of Christian faith was to be found in the promises of the future. Consequently he devoted much of his ministry to teaching about the specific developments that he felt were foretold. Though the book speaks to a different part of my thinking and feeling, so that it is not necessary for my spiritual stability to be reminded that God is going to justify all historical wrongs in one cataclysmic act, I recognize that some people have to see it that way to be able to hope. Certainly John of Patmos knew that there were many different kinds of people to be ministered to by his writings, and his message was for all. Some of us have farther to come through the tunnels of our soul to daylight, and any kind of lantern that brightens our journey to the next corner is to the good.

This is what the city foursquare brings to light. We dream it in different ways, but it is essentially the same dream. Some of us are frightened and dream of an order in which we are protected, secure, assured that we will not be victimized by others. Some of us are lonely, and our dream looks to a city of acceptance and affection. Some of us have unused reserves of energy and concern, and yearn for opportunities to relate in outgoing love and trust. Some of us would just like to see some arrangement somewhere where ideas and concepts, law and public morality, are so visibly successful that we can depend on life's being what it's supposed to be.

Some of us are sick, dismayed at our own distortion of the good, and even depressed and hopeless. Though the dream is here much less specific, it still is a cry for healing and renewal. The city foursquare is the pictorial confirmation that being healed is of the nature and destiny of man, and no matter how blurred our own capacity to hope may be, we were created to be whole.

It is therefore understandable that there are dynamically diverse ways of dealing with the details of the invitation to hope. As far as I'm concerned, it would be most desirable if the church reverberated daily with the promises and celebrated with joy. It's not at all a serious sin to have to react to the symbols according to our contextual preparation; it would be a far worse predicament for a symbol of hope to become a reason for disunity. Embarrassed tolerance is no substitute for joy. It is the gladness in having a basis for hope that gives us reason to stand together.

Again quoting Harvey Cox: "At the center of the Christian message is the fact of a Kingdom which is always coming, which has never fully arrived, and which therefore provides a constant basis for our hope. The Christian is one who is oriented toward the future and whose posture of hopeful expectation, though it may be disappointed from time to time, is never fully defeated."

To paraphrase Rev. 21:15-21:

> I found that I could not help but marvel
> That God put man together in communities,
> And that like a crystal,
> A snowflake,
> There is always a basic order,

A symmetry,
A design,
Feebly reflected wherever men covenant together
For mutual good.
And this order, sometimes visible, sometimes dim,
Made me want to be so much in it
That I felt its beauty could indeed prevail.
And then I knew
That where community exists
There is an indescribable mystery locked
And someday it will be freed,
And I was glad to be in the city.

No Temple in the City (*Rev. 21:22*). Thank God the church is only transitional, temporary! It is not an end in itself; it is only an instrument that God uses to effect his will! The biggest danger of all for anybody today is that of idolatry, which is defined as worshiping as supreme anything that is less than God. We become like the gods we follow, and the idolater is the slave of inhumanity if his god is inhuman. But for the Christian the temptation is even more perilous—to make an idolatry of the church itself, to impute holiness on a structure and sanctity toward the undeserving.

An enterprising church executive had his stationery imprinted with the words, "The Church Exists for Those Outside Itself." To his surprise, there was such a clamor of objections from his colleagues that he had to change it. Why is it so startling to say that a tool is fulfilling its purpose when it is used for the task? Yet in that day when God reigns in every heart, the church will be quite unnecessary, for all creation will be itself a worshiping community, and the things that are eternally true will be the subjects of our common speech.

But this is neither a new concept, nor unusual. Our

mission strategy has always been to be the dispensable innovator. Where there are those who do not see the spiritual implications of physical healing, the church has founded hospitals and clinics and then as quickly as possible turned them over to government or indigenous leaders. Likewise with schools and community organizations, labor unions and movements for dignity, rights, housing, and justice. Every movement toward the exaltation of the wholeness of man should be secular, from the whole core of community life, looking to that day when society is virtuous and there is no temple there. Somehow, that gives me both a reason to plunge into the church with redoubled effort and an ability to take its imperfections less seriously. "After all," I can say to it, "someday we're going to get along without you."

The Time Is Near—I Am Coming Soon (*Rev. 22:12*). Well, there you have it. The Christian is an unapologetic believer in this world, in all its beauty and garbage, its loveliness and disgrace, its promise and its bitterness. He just can't help but be, because his faith leads him to understand something of the fabric of its purpose, but even more, to know that he is known by the Creator.

Theologians don't really know very much about God. Nor does the church, for all its years of worshiping and teaching. As a matter of fact, nobody knows enough about God to be anything close to authoritative. We don't know a thing about his nature, his power, or his will. The difference between a scholarly preacher and the most indifferent agnostic in their wisdom about God is really not very much at all.

But the church doesn't have to know. God never seems to have required that at all. He provided us with a series of redemptive experiences and relationships. He led us through a series of wildernesses and then came and sat on our doorstep in the evening cool in Jesus Christ, patted us on the shoulder and said, "Keep the faith." No, we don't know very much about him. But we do know a great deal about man and about what man needs in order to be whole. The Christian faith is, then, at the roots, an attitude toward life and self that revels in joy and forgiveness and sees the divine spark in all His children.

Hope is simply translating that sensation of being accepted into the circumstances we have to deal with, expecting it to be worthwhile. In April of 1958, the secretariat staff of the United Nations gave a surprise party for their recently reelected Secretary General, Dag Hammarskjöld. In the impromptu speech that Hammarskjöld gave that day he quoted the Swedish poet Gunnar Ekelof, "Will the day ever come when joy is great and sorrow small?" to which Hammarskjöld added his own answer, "On the day we feel we are living with a duty, well fulfilled and worth our while, on that day joy is great and we can look on sorrow as being small."

It's really a rather exciting time to be alive. Everything, but *everything* is up for grabs, and no institution, including the church and your family, is impregnably secure. But, as Cox affirms, "When all else is said and done the church is a people who celebrate and hope. . . . If people around us think this seems a little crazy it will not be the first time the followers of Christ have been marked down as fools."